Hot Tips, Sneaky Tricks, and Last-Ditch Tactics

Hot Tips, Sneaky Tricks, and Last-Ditch Tactics

An Insider's Guide to Getting Your First Corporate Job

Jeff B. Speck

WILEY

John Wiley & Sons

New York   Chichester   Brisbane   Toronto   Singapore

Library of Congress Cataloging in Publication Data:

Speck, Jeff B.

   Hot tips, sneaky tricks, and last-ditch tactics: an insider's
   guide to getting your first corporate job / Jeff B. Speck
      p.   cm.
   Bibliography: p.
   ISBN 0-471-61514-5
   1. Job hunting—United States.   2. Employment
interviewing—United States.   3. College graduates—
Employment—United States.
I. Title.
HF5382.75.U6S64   1989   88-28699
650.1'4—dc19   CIP

Printed in the United States of America

10 9 8 7 6 5 4 3 2 1

Preface

Alas, what has become of America's youth? Whereas idealistic college seniors once flocked after graduation—or quit school early—to join the Peace Corps, march on Washington, or otherwise make an impact on society, now it seems that all they want to do is land corporate jobs and make big money. Open rejection of the previous generation's values was once the norm; now the updated definition of *child rebellion* involves participating in a hostile takeover of one's parents' corporation.

Although corporate positions were at one time an easy opportunity for those few ardent capitalists who *actually wanted them,* now a limited number of prestigious jobs are actively sought by an ever increasing army of would-be robber barons. And who can resist, at age twenty-one, the opportunity to pay over ten-thousand dollars in income tax?

As a result, the attitude among corporate recruiters is one of complete advantage. You would have to serve on a hiring committee to understand the total, luxurious—perhaps arrogant—sense of unmitigated power that exists there. As one colleague of mine put it: "Having your *gluteus maximus* kissed by a never ending stream of the 'best and the brightest' can't help but have an effect on you." Keeping this in mind, and understanding that a recruiter is under almost constant pressure to eliminate as many candidates as possible, you must approach the challenge with every advantage attainable.

That is where this book comes in handy. It is not intended to be a didactic, comprehensive primer on job-hunting. Rather, it is one person's subjective account of how to survive the corporate recruiting process. Since it is based almost entirely on first-hand experience, the information contained herein is not equally applicable to all industries. You will find this book most useful if you are looking for a job in banking, consulting, accounting, insurance, real estate, or the Fortune 500. I have sacrificed scope for focus in order to present my advice as that of an insider rather than a researcher. Of course, if used in a general sense, this book can help you no matter what type of job you are seeking.

I went through the corporate recruiting process as a college senior and managed to land a job as an analyst with a large investment bank in New York. One year later I found myself named a coordinator of analyst recruiting, ready, willing, and able to turn the tables on however many hapless youths happened to stumble my way. In that position, I learned how lucky I was to have landed any job at all, and how hiring decisions were based on a myriad of factors, many not entirely rational, that I had never before considered. Most importantly, I realized the cause of my previous ignorance: the utter lack of publications addressing the specific topic from the inside out. In the face of a plethora of job-hunting books either too generic to be of any help or written by outsiders looking in, I decided to publish my experience for those aspiring to hop on the corporate bandwagon.

This is the only book written from the perspective of a hiring decision-maker who is himself recently out of college. As such, it is the only book that knows not only the answers that come from making employment decisions, but also the questions that a college student or recent graduate needs to have answered. I remember, when I was interviewing for jobs, how I would try to put myself in the shoes of my interviewers and figure out what

they were thinking, how they were judging me, and what I could
do to elicit a positive response. A year later I found out. This
book will teach you what I learned, as an interviewee-turned-
interviewer and judged-turned-judge, about what it takes to get
a corporate job today.

So, to risk sounding like a corporate recruiter: "How badly do
you want it?" If you go to the trouble—and it's not much
trouble—of following the steps outlined here, you can't help
but have the edge. As you will see, that edge may be necessary.

I would suggest that you read the complete book before
embarking on the job-hunting process and then reread the
appropriate chapters as you move ahead. An index is provided
at the back for last-minute emergencies.

JEFF B. SPECK

New York, New York
February 1989

Acknowledgments

Many thanks to: Bruce Albelda, Sam Broeksmit, Joan Curhan, Maggie and Melanie Dana, Mike Hamilton, Rob Kirkpatrick, Maryan Malone, John Raybin, Holden Shannon, Debbie and Martha Wickenden, Adam Wilson, Kathy Woodruff, and—especially—Nancy Zughaib and the Speck family.

Disclaimer

Like many nonfiction writers, I have found it necessary to sacrifice gender neutrality in favor of verbal clarity. When the word *he* is used generally, it is intended to signify *he or she*. Until a less awkward neuter pronoun is invented, I do not see that authors have much choice. If anyone has any good ideas on this topic, he or she should write his or her congress-man/woman and ask him or her to get cracking on it.

Contents

Hot Tips, Sneaky Tricks, and
Last-Ditch Tactics

1

The Process, the Jobs

Use the System

You're lucky: The corporate recruiting process is surprisingly standardized, especially among the larger firms that are accustomed to hiring college seniors and recent graduates for their entry-level positions. Each corporation may have its idiosyncracies, but most companies follow the same general procedure when it comes to determining which applicants become employees. This makes your job hunting much easier, as a single strategy can spell success at a number of different firms.

You will quickly learn that the recruiting process at most of these corporations runs as follows: résumé review, first-round "screen" interview, second-round "callback" interview, and final decision. At some firms, a third-round interview is necessary for them to reach a decision. (This is usually company policy and does not reflect badly on you.) That's the system.

I should warn you now that this book addresses the topic of success *within that system.* It will not tell you how to get around it—getting around it is almost impossible—but, rather, how to make it work for you.

There are, of course, less orthodox approaches to getting a job, but they are generally not effective in landing *this type* of job. Those approaches utilize such strategies as relying entirely on contacts and casting the résumé aside (in which case you need quick feet to dodge résumé requests). That might be fine for working your way into a small company with no formal recruiting procedure, but it won't get you very far in the big leagues. At my firm it was as simple as: "No résumé, no job." Contacts could earn you an interview, but you had to earn the offer yourself.

This book is about *getting a job*, not *deciding what job to get*, so I will not dwell on the choice of where to look. You have probably already made your decision. But, for those of you who are still looking for advice: It's true that working for some big-name firms can have its disadvantages, most notably, a lack of responsibility and upward mobility in some cases. But, first of all, I should mention that these are simply generalizations. I could not have handled any more responsibility and career-advancement opportunity than I was provided by my entry-level investment banking job. Secondly, even with the possibility of those disadvantages in mind, there are a number of compelling reasons supporting your decision to aim for the sort of fast-track job you are considering.

Your first job is most important in that it gets you your second job. If your first job is with a well-known, respected company, you will find yourself in a truly advantageous position when it comes time to look elsewhere. When your résumé is read, when your candidacy is discussed, even when you are introduced, your job becomes a part of you, almost an appendix to your name, like "Ph. D." Your second job—typically the job in which people join the field where they will spend their careers—will be that much easier to get if your first job has the advantage of quick, positive name recognition.

And the benefit doesn't stop there; the big-name firm stays on your résumé forever. Even twenty years down the road, it will still be there to lend credibility to your candidacy.

You may be thinking: "Why do it now? Why not join a name-recognition firm in a few years? Either way, it will be on my résumé." The fact is, however, that there may never be an easier time than now to do so. Most elitist companies, for their entry-level positions, won't hire people who are over twenty-five or who have spent more than two years working for some unknown private business. It's one thing to have taught English in a private school or worked as a park ranger, but "inferior" *corporate* experience can make you undesirable to the big names, who are looking for fresh, unspoiled talent.

And let's not forget that there are, should you want them, quite lucrative long-term careers available with these companies. The best way to start a career with Citicorp is to get a job with Citicorp. But that's enough on that subject; the choice is yours. For perhaps the only time in this book, I will *not* tell you what to do.

2

The Résumé and Cover Letter

Elimination-Avoidance Maneuvers

Sorting through résumés is the easiest chore for the recruiter, and thus is the step in the process at which errors are almost guaranteed to be lethal. The decision-maker can whimsically eliminate hundreds of qualified candidates and still be left with too many to interview. You have perhaps heard horror stories about recruiters who toss a pile of résumés into the air and automatically discard all that do not land face up.

While this sort of thing rarely happens, most people would accept it as an accurate approximation of the selection process. All recruiter randomness aside, the keys to getting through the average résumé review process are straightforward: Appear qualified, make no obvious errors, and distinguish yourself without turning people off or scaring them away.

The Selection Process

When a firm is preparing for college interviews, there are usually three or four people involved in the résumé-sort: two members of the official recruiting committee, one of whom will be interviewing on campus; a second campus interviewer, typically an alumnus; and perhaps one more alumnus who wants a chance to wreak revenge on his old school. For "walk-on" candidates—college graduates and seniors at schools that the firm doesn't visit—there are usually two or three young professionals who alone decide whom to invite for an office interview.

Each member of the review team receives copies of all the résumés and reviews them independently, ranking them from top to bottom, or at least dividing them into four or five groups based upon perceived "hireability." A few days later the group convenes and compares selections by noting the mutual favorites and squabbling over the not-so-mutual favorites until all of the interview slots are filled.

Although many a candidate's fate is determined in the selection meeting, the dynamics of that situation are far beyond the candidate's control. All an applicant should worry about is impressing each decision-maker independently.

Who is your audience? At this point in the process it is unlikely that any senior members of your target firms are even remotely involved. At least half of your reviewers are probably working in the very position for which you are applying, and the others are no higher than middle management. One, or more at the largest firms, may be from the personnel department. They have all seen quite a few résumés, and certainly remember their own from not very long ago.

These people may find the screening of résumés tedious, but the reviewers who are not from the personnel department probably consider it a nice interruption from more routine work. For the younger decision-makers, the job also provides some weighty responsibility at a time when they are relegated primarily to support roles.

Each reviewer develops his own technique for sorting through résumés, and rarely is he instructed on how to do so. Some reviewers, unsurprisingly, simply look for similarities between their own background and those of the applicants they are screening. However, I have found that the method followed does not differ significantly among firms or reviewers, including myself. Here is the system I have developed for turning a pile of two hundred résumés into twenty favorites.

Step One: Eliminate the Losers   This part is by far the most fun. It involves a single sort through the pile, in which my goal is to throw out at least half of the résumés. I first assess my own attitude before embarking on this task, making certain that I feel no charity toward anyone. At this stage applicants find their way into the *reject* pile either by not demonstrating the qualifications for the job or by making obvious mistakes.

Errors—grammatical or stylistic—are entirely inexcusable in a process as competitive as this one. Most of the mistakes that I find take the form of inconsistencies: unwarranted changes in verb tense, punctuation, and capitalization. Even layout inconsistencies, while sometimes tolerable, can be cause for rejection. And as much as people may warn each other about it, someone always spells *liaison* wrong.

While the assessment of qualifications is a more subjective task, my colleagues and I have managed to divide our rating criteria into four categories: academic standing, previous work experience, extracurricular activity, and likely interest in the job. More detail on each category is given at the end of this section.

If the candidate does not qualify in at least two of the categories, I can remove his résumé from my pile on the first round. If I do my job well, I am left with fewer than seventy-five résumés out of the original two-hundred.

Step Two: Comparisons   At this point, I am able to gather a sense of the general quality of the résumés. If I am lucky, I may find that many candidates score high in three of the four categories that I am investigating, in which case I can again eliminate those who don't measure up.

I also begin to look more closely at the quality of the document itself. At some schools, for example, students do not have access to typesetting facilities or personal computers, in which case I forgive a typewritten résumé. However, a typewritten résumé amidst a pile of typeset ones can't help projecting a lack of desire for the job. Computer word-processed résumés are usually fine, unless done in **take me to your leader** type or on a weak dot-matrix printer. There still exists some dispute among recruiters, but I believe that Apple Macintosh-modeled résumés are fine as long as they are printed on a laser printer.

Two more quick reviews allow me to toss those that no longer comply with the toughening standards. Eventually I am left with about thirty or forty résumés of excellent quality, from which I have to pick twenty.

Step Three: Personal Preferences   By this stage, I have inevitably found the five "stars" in the pile—the campus leaders, well-rounded 4.0s, and entrepreneurs worth half a million dollars—and set them aside as definites.

It really doesn't matter which of the remaining candidates I now choose; I truly cannot distinguish who is likely to be a good hire. However, the ones whom I do not choose will not even be mentioned in the selection meeting (unless by someone else), so this point is a crucial one for the applicant. This is when the reviewer starts to think, "Who do I like here?" and when it is important to have something on your résumé that, very subtly, differentiates you.

The safe approach is to list something unusual or otherwise interesting under your extracurricular activities or job experience. If you have done something worthwhile that sets you apart from the rest, be sure to mention it. Good examples are starting a campus club, teaching a mini-course, or coaching a team. Your chance of arousing the recruiter's interest will also improve as you move away from the confines of campus life. Community activity or other volunteer work would often win my approval.

And, believe it or not, *fun* activities are also smiled upon. One candidate I met held a summer job as Goofy at Disneyland. *Everybody* gave him interviews.

If you come up empty in this category, the other solution is to include a "Personal" section at the bottom of your résumé. This is a touchy area, and it must be approached carefully as it can often cause more problems than it solves.

For example, traveling around the world is impressive if it is in the form of solo backpacking or bicycling, but if done as a guest of wealthy parents it is grounds for rejection. For this very reason, I am a strong believer that a "Personal" paragraph should only be used if you absolutely need to distinguish yourself further. (I can't tell you how many "Enjoy tennis, skiing" sentences I have read.)

Some good and bad personal items follow, should you feel the need to use that dangerous format.

ASSETS

Play jai-alai
Write and perform jazz music
Certified SCUBA diver
Avid cook

Bridge player
Black belt in Tae kwon-do
Ski instructor

*COACH LITTLE LEAGUE
or
SOCCER
or
?*

LIABILITIES

Play touch football
Enjoy listening to music
Yachting
Enjoy fine dining
Cosmetologist
Marital status: single
5' 9", 145 lbs., good health

Just from the interests they list, I get the impression that the applicants in the first group are unusual, creative, adventurous, inventive, analytical, disciplined, and hearty, while those in the second group are commonplace, lazy, privileged, spoiled, ditzy, regimented, and boring. This may not be true, but the truth doesn't matter; the impression matters. Hopefully these examples give you a good sense of the DOs and DON'Ts of writing a "Personal" paragraph. Once again: Avoid it if you can.

Deciding who I *like the most* out of these résumés cuts my number to twenty, and now the original two hundred have been divided into five piles:

1. Five "stars"
2. Fifteen other interviewees
3. Fifteen qualifiers who didn't make the final cut
4. Forty second-round rejects
5. One hundred and twenty-five original rejects.

If I have done my job well, only the candidates in the first two piles are likely to get an interview. The candidates in pile three stand a chance only if the other reviewers find them extremely interesting.

Academic Standing

While every participant in the recruiting process has a different concept of the importance of grades—typically derived from his own college performance—they are a significant factor in selecting candidates. Academic standing may not be the most important of selection criteria, but because it is so easily quantifiable, it often serves as a basis for candidate elimination. The most natural step in narrowing down a pile of résumés is to toss out all of those applicants whose GPAs do not reach a certain level.

Recruiters are generally more willing to forgive average grades if they belong to students who have technical majors or come from prestigious colleges. If you are applying from an environment that is not especially rigorous, grades become much more important.

Unfortunately, it is not a guaranteed solution to leave a low grade point average off your résumé, since it has become standard practice for students with GPAs above 3.2 to say so. Having no mention of your GPA therefore

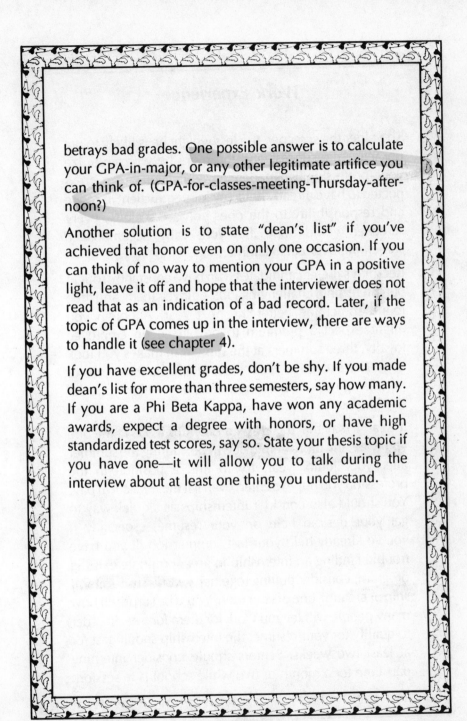

betrays bad grades. One possible answer is to calculate your GPA-in-major, or any other legitimate artifice you can think of. (GPA-for-classes-meeting-Thursday-afternoon?)

Another solution is to state "dean's list" if you've achieved that honor even on only one occasion. If you can think of no way to mention your GPA in a positive light, leave it off and hope that the interviewer does not read that as an indication of a bad record. Later, if the topic of GPA comes up in the interview, there are ways to handle it (see chapter 4).

If you have excellent grades, don't be shy. If you made dean's list for more than three semesters, say how many. If you are a Phi Beta Kappa, have won any academic awards, expect a degree with honors, or have high standardized test scores, say so. State your thesis topic if you have one—it will allow you to talk during the interview about at least one thing you understand.

Work Experience

The older the screener, the less weight he is likely to put on academic success and the more he will scrutinize your professional experience. While you are not expected to have already held any jobs equivalent in scope and responsibility to the ones you are seeking, every screener would hope that you really *accomplished something* over each summer.

Recruiters prefer candidates who have constantly sought out interesting, challenging jobs, enjoyed them, and then found something better the next year. Although you might expect a premium to be placed on employee loyalty, three summers at the same firm makes you look lazy. The exception, of course, would be three jobs of increasing responsibility at a company within your desired industry.

It is fair to say that the closer a previous job is to the one you want, the more helpful it will be. During the summer after your junior year, try to find a position in the profession you hope to enter, even if it means a cut in pay. You should also consider internships as a quick way to get your desired field on your résumé, especially if you've already held your last summer job. If you have trouble landing an internship in an appropriate existing program, consider putting together a work–study internship or creating one of your own. You'd be surprised how many people will let you work for them for free. In order to qualify for your résumé, the internship should last for at least two weeks. Seniors should consider interning part-time for a month or two while school is in session.

When reviewing résumés, I look for at least two "real" jobs (*i.e.*, work that involves a significant amount of thought) and perhaps one "roll-up-the-sleeves" job, such as bartending or landscaping, preferably several years ago. Sales experience, even door-to-door, always impresses me. And long hours are also an incredible help; if you have worked sixty hours per week, say so.

Don't waste valuable space telling recruiters that as a secretary you performed, "basic secretarial functions such as typing, copying, and answering the telephone"—it's obvious. Instead, focus on the parts of the job that made it unique or how you excelled within the position. Specific examples lend credibility to your story.

Try to use the active voice, and avoid using similar words in each description. Stay away from the words that everyone else is using—*liaison* is one of them.

Unusual jobs that may not be applicable to the position you seek are definitely worth mentioning if they are interesting. As a senior, I probably owed half of my investment banking interviews to the fact that I had spent one summer teaching astronomy. Another big plus is entrepreneurial work, as long as you don't call it that. Do not mention McDonald's or Burger King unless you worked there more than two years ago and were a shift manager or better. (Trust me on this one.)

Extracurricular Activity

Recruiters look to extracurricular activity to manifest four things about a candidate: energy level, leadership skills, team-playing abilities, and an interest in something other than soap operas, MTV, and professional wrestling. List your activities with these criteria in mind.

Extracurriculars are also where one can find evidence of a person's "star" quality. There is no substitute for being Ms. Three-Sport Captain or Mr. Campus Leader. In the absence of a deep involvement in one or two nonacademic activities, however, superficial participation in a large number of groups can also be impressive, particularly if they have something to do with the job you want. It helps to list your activities with no mention of their dates or duration; that way, they all appear simultaneous.

A word of warning: Every campus has its bogus organizations that have been created by seniors to impress corporate recruiters. Before you list such a do-nothing affiliation on your résumé (if you must), be certain that no recent alumni of your school will be reviewing it.

Interest in the Job

This is most easily handled in an interview, but to get that opportunity you must drop a few hints on your résumé. Job interest can best be implied on a résumé by mentioning applicable course work, extracurricular activity, or professional experience.

I am strongly against the use of "Objective" statements atop a résumé unless an applicant has only one objective and it's a specific one. Printing three résumés with three different objectives is a sleazy practice and one at which you can easily get caught. Your cover letter should state your objective plainly, so the only reason I can think of for putting it on your résumé is to use up space. (And who needs to do that?) The worst are the ones that talk about "making full use of my skills and abilities." Yucko.

If you decide that your résumé needs a "Personal" section, that's another place to indicate an interest in the job. If you are looking for a job with a real-estate developer, for example, mentioning an interest in such related areas as architecture and urbanism will get the point across.

References

You are probably planning to say "References available upon request" at the bottom of your résumé. Go ahead, if you have the space, but it's unnecessary; if your reviewers want references, they'll ask for them. (They rarely do.)

Since you are unlikely to be asked for references, any work you do in that area is probably a waste of time. However, you do need to be prepared for the possibility, so it is dangerous to ignore the issue completely. Once you start getting interviews, ask a former employer and favorite professor if they would be willing to serve as your references. Fill them in on your job-search plans. Then send them a copy of your résumé, along with a quick note that says that they probably won't be bothered.

It's fine to stop there, unless you find out that calls to your references are imminent. Then you would be wise to contact them immediately and let them know who will be calling. Tell them a little bit about the company and why you want to work there. Ask them if they would like any more information on the aspects of your record that they are not familiar with.

Of course, if someone is writing you a letter of recommendation (see page 30), he is a perfect reference. Then you only need to locate one more. Do not waste a lot of time on this task, and if you're extremely busy it should not be a high priority.

A Final Word on Résumés

A résumé is not something to be taken on single-handedly. To get started, you should definitely consult at least one book on résumé preparation. That book should be a standard, respected guide, not anything newfangled that reads like *Knock 'Em Dead with a Whacko Résumé.* Be suspicious of any book that recommends business résumés exceeding one page in length.

Also elicit the help of your friends, parents, guidance counselor (even if you've graduated), and any connections you have in the business world. Working with a neatly typed rough draft, get as much advice as you can in a week or two, *and then stop.* After a while your sources will begin to contradict each other, and then you'll have to trust your own judgment. When choosing between contradictory bits of advice, always favor the person in the industry over the person in the guidance office.

The seventies are history, and so are "results-oriented" résumés and letter résumés. They may be effective in other fields or at higher levels, but they are not considered acceptable by conventional corporate recruiters. You will get the best results if you stick to a biographical format.

Some guides suggest sending along photographs or, worse yet, "head shots," in which your résumé is printed on the back of an 8½-x-11-inch glossy portrait of you-know-who. I wouldn't believe it if I hadn't read it. Unless you're looking for a spot on "Dynasty," I suggest you ignore that advice.

Generally, the more well-rounded you appear, the better. You don't want to come across as one-dimensional, even if that one dimension is business. If you do not have a strong business background, you are wise to make the most of whatever related experience you do have. But if you are a business, finance, economics, or accounting major, you have to stress the factors that make you unusual.

Finally, don't put anything on your résumé that you wouldn't be able to explain impressively during an interview. I once interviewed a recent graduate from the Ivy League whose main activity for the past six months had been "Independent Film Study." When I asked him what that study entailed, he responded, "Well, I'd rent movies from the video store and watch them on the VCR over and over again . . . really carefully, you know?" Others may have been able to explain it better, but that "activity" doomed him to failure.

Walk-Ons

If you are not a student at a college where one of your target firms collects résumés and/or conducts interviews, you qualify as a "walk-on." You may have graduated several years ago, or you may currently attend a college that does not draw recruiters from some or all of the big-name corporations. In either case, a similar situation prevails: The firms that interest you have decided that their entry-level employment needs can be met elsewhere, probably by recruiting seniors from ten or twenty choice colleges. A candidate with your background represents a peripheral addition to the process.

As an aberration of sorts, you will find yourself with a bit more work to do and a number of additional choices to make. This does not mean, however, that you are any worse off because of it.

The first question you face is whether to approach these firms through their college recruiting system or through some other function. The fact is that most other avenues toward an offer, such as the want ads or the personnel department, are primarily geared toward hiring secretaries, technicians, and upper-level management. Most large firms have discovered that the place to go for intelligent, unspoiled, entry-level workers is college. As a veritable *tabula rasa*—a college graduate with few specific job skills—you have little to gain by taking any other path (unless you can work your way in through connections or information interviews). In fact, many firms, if they don't toss you aside, will refer you to their campus recruiters no matter what channels you apply through.

The problem with becoming a part of the college draft is that you are immediately presented with a tremendous amount of competition. Wouldn't it be better, perhaps, to wait until summer, when the college recruiting season is over, and *then* try to find a job? The answer is no, only because firms that complete successful college recruiting seasons will not make many offers in the off-season; they have already met their hiring needs. If you already have your eye on a specific firm, you probably cannot afford to wait.

Joining the college draft is not as bad as you think. Your competition in the toughest part of the process, the résumé-sort, will probably be only the other walk-ons. This is because the résumés received are so plentiful that most firms do their résumé-sorting and interviewing school by school. Since you are not affiliated with any of the schools designated, you will probably end up in a walk-on pile, which is often smaller than most of the others.

And there are other factors at work. Theoretically, companies have certain universal standards concerning who is worthy of an interview. But, as described earlier in this chapter, most colleges send along more than enough qualified résumés, and the number of interviews at each college is strictly limited by the number of people the firm can send to campus. Since walk-on candidates interview at the company's offices, there is probably no set limit to the number of these applicants that are granted interviews. So, not only is your pile smaller—and probably less competitive as well—but more interviews also result from it.

It is a fact that many of the college students my firm rejected last year would have made it as walk-ons. If a company is in the habit of interviewing walk-ons, the walk-on pile may be the safest place for a qualified résumé.

Recent Graduates of Solicited Colleges Bearing the previous discussion in mind, if you are a recent graduate of a school that *is* solicited for résumés, then you probably want to avoid being classified with the undergraduates. If you went to the University of Pennsylvania, for example, being placed with the current seniors would perhaps give you as many as five hundred U. Penn résumés as competition. You would do much better in a pile of two hundred résumés from a wide variety of schools. Many firms will automatically review the graduates separately, but the only way to ensure that you are kept out of your alma mater's résumé pile is to delay submitting your résumé until the school's selections have already been made.

The campus career counseling office will be able to tell you when this has occurred, and then you should forward your résumé immediately. This practice only becomes dangerous, thus inadvisable, toward the end of the season, when callback interviews are already in progress.

An opposite strategy would apply if you have graduated from a small school that is nonetheless visited by a company that interests you. If the current class of seniors does not pose stiff competition, try to land yourself an on-campus interview. Either through the career counseling office or independently, have your résumé arrive with those from this year's class. (Make sure that it goes to the same person.) In your cover letter, mention that you are a recent graduate and are willing to interview either on campus or at their offices.

Of course, if you find out that a firm simply does not conduct walk-on interviews, this approach would be your only choice, aside from the *connections* route.

Seniors at, and Graduates of, Unsolicited Colleges If your school does not interest your most-wanted firms, you are deprived of the career counseling office's information flow. Thus, a bit more research is required on your part. Don't be afraid of the telephone—a few calls will let you know whether walk-ons are welcome and where to send your résumé. Call the division that interests you (through the main switchboard) and ask for the professional who typically handles recruiting for the position you seek. If that doesn't work, ask to speak to someone holding that position—he will be sure to know who's in charge.

Don't speak to the personnel department if you can help it. They will tell you, in a bland monotone, "Send your résumé to us." That puts an additional level of screening between you and the job. Even if they like you, by the time they pass your résumé upstairs, you could be running your own company.

Despite your apprehension, most people will not be annoyed by a quick phone call. As long as you are cheerful and concise, they will probably appreciate the interruption. Perhaps the only exception to this rule would be the trading floors at brokerage firms, but even those tend to get friendlier in the late afternoon. Before you call, find out how the market did that day.

If all of your research still fails to locate the person who screens résumés, send yours to someone senior in the firm (below CEO). A résumé passed down from a superior is often assumed to have connections and to deserve special treatment.

If you are applying for a job at a company that gets hundreds of walk-on résumés a week, you know you have to do something different to get an interview. Don't write a crazy letter; just try to work your way in through a different approach. Connections and information interviewing may be your only route in this situation.

The Off-Season Even in the hiring off-season, which usually runs from July to December, positions are definitely available. There may not be many openings at the firms that most interest you, but, for the firms that *are* hiring, your chances are better now than at any other time. Like the seniors at unsolicited colleges, you now need only determine whether it's worth sending in your résumé and where to send it.

Though friends are helpful at every point in the process, they can come in especially handy here. Due to the disorganized nature of most off-season hiring practices, a much larger percentage of the jobs available go to people with connections. When the head of the off-season recruiting effort at my firm was a recent Princeton graduate, was it mere coincidence that half of the people hired were from Princeton as well? Especially if you've been out of school for a couple of years, you are very likely to have one or two friends at some of the corporations that interest you. Find them.

Of course, the biggest reason that friends play such an influential role in off-season hiring is that they can notify you if an opening exists. Their influence on the process would be greatly diminished if more *unconnected* job-hunters were willing to do the footwork to find the openings. Don't use your lack of contacts as an excuse until you've made all of the necessary phone calls.

Get Real

When you are deciding what jobs to go after—and what industries to eliminate as "undesirable"—be sure not to restrict yourself to jobs that you don't have a realistic chance of getting. Select a group of opportunities that are all potentially within reach, as well as a couple of back-ups in case your plans go awry. At the end of the recruiting season, you at least will have a temporary place to work if you need one, and you won't be forced to leech off your parents while looking for a better opportunity.

Some overambitious students put in a tremendous six-month job-hunting effort which not only is a waste of time but also keeps them too busy to apply for jobs that they have a chance of getting. After a jobless graduation, they are faced with the prospect of starting all over again.

Don't make the same mistake. Look at your résumé, yourself, and your competition, and decide exactly where you stand. Pick a good friend who seems to have his act together and ask his opinion on what level of job you deserve. Ultimately, you can usually count on someone in the career counseling office to give you the straight scoop on your chances, even if you've already graduated. Don't sell yourself short, but don't waste your time.

After assessing your candidacy, you may decide nonetheless to try for some jobs that seem over your head. Because you know that you are at a disadvantage, you can now take appropriate action. Write a letter to a vice president or try to work your way in through an information interview. It may not work, but you've got nothing to lose.

Connections

Connections are your number one resource, period. What you have already read of this chapter makes one thing clear: If you can somehow get around the résumé-screening process, you should do so. And connections are the only legitimate way to jump quickly over this most difficult step in getting a job.

There are two types of connections: those you have and those you make. The former are more helpful, but both are worth taking advantage of.

Connections You Have   The best connections you can have, due to their likely seniority, are friends of parents and parents of friends. These people are at just the right age to be running companies, or at least departments. You may not think that you know anyone of this stature, but are you sure? Uncles and aunts are worth considering as well. One may be all that it takes.

If you do locate such a person, you must decide whether you know him well enough to ask for a real favor. If he was around when you were growing up or if you've spent any nights under his roof, then you are probably not out of line asking him to pull some strings for you. If your relationship is more superficial, it would be best to play it safe and start with an information interview (see chapter 3). If he wants to be more helpful, he will probably make it obvious.

Once a connection offers to lend a hand, solicit his help in determining the next move. If he pulls some weight in an organization that interests you, chances are the best next move is simply an interview. Your likelihood of getting an interview depends primarily on that person's title. When I was making interview decisions at my firm, vice presidents would ask me, "If this person qualifies, could you interview him?" Managing directors would just say, "Jeff, I want this person to get an interview."

If your connection is not in your desired industry, he could still be incredibly valuable. Does he do business with anyone in that industry? A firm's clients are often a lot more powerful than its officers. I almost had to *hire* someone once, just because he knew an important client. If your uncle is Chief Financial Officer at Ford, there isn't one accounting company, investment bank, or law firm that won't give you an interview.

Friends of yours who have recently graduated can also be quite helpful. If they are two years out of college, they may very well be running recruiting campaigns, and even last year's graduates are probably doing some interviewing. While these junior executives are generally averse to abusing their authority, they'll gladly do it for a good friend.

Once again, you have to determine whether their primary allegiance lies with the company or with you. If you lived or frequently socialized with a recent graduate, you can expect him to be on your side. But if an old "friend" has been working for two years and you two haven't spoken since graduation, be careful. You'd be surprised how quickly someone can become a corporate tool.

Communicate with your friends by telephone, at home if possible; written correspondence makes you look like just another applicant. If you are fairly certain that a friend would want to get you an interview, go ahead and ask. Otherwise, just ask for advice and see where that leads you. If nothing better materializes, settle for an information interview.

Your college faculty is another potential source of connections. Economics and business professors often have significant ties to the private sector. Many are taking some time off from high-powered corporate jobs, and others work part-time as consultants. The problem with turning to them for help is that they are equally accessible to hundreds of other students, so you can't expect them to do you any special favors. Typically, they are most valuable as sources of information.

The exception would be professors with whom you have developed a personal relationship, or those who regard you as their star pupil. If you consider them more likely to help you than most other students, they are definitely worth approaching. Also, since many students neglect to access the faculty for job-hunting assistance, these professors may not be as burdened by requests as you think.

Connections You Make For the most part, these are businesspeople with whom you are already connected—they just don't know it yet. Alumni of your college, members of your fraternity or sorority, professionals who live in your neighborhood or go to your church—these people might be willing to assist someone who shares an aspect of their background.

The most that you can probably expect from them at first is an information interview, but that may lead to better things. Once they get to know you, they could end up being as helpful as a family member.

You're responsible for finding out who does what in your community, but most colleges and some fraternities and sororities have alumni directories that can lead you to the right people. Don't be shy; if you tell them where you found their name, they can hardly resent your call.

Letters of Recommendation

In applying for jobs, you may have considered sending a letter of recommendation along with your résumé and cover letter. This is far from established practice, but it is done now and then and can be very helpful if done intelligently.

In order to be worth mailing, your letter of recommendation must be one of two things: either a positive note written by a person who is well known in the industry, or a glowing essay by someone with a respected title in a legitimate organization.

In the first case, you are relying on name recognition to do the trick. Your goal is to elicit a response like, "Well, if Porter likes this guy, he must be worth talking to." The letter need not be lengthy or extremely enthusiastic, as long as it's affirmative. Of course, the more enthusiastic the letter, the better. If you have worked with someone whom your reviewers have probably heard of, this is an excellent option.

In the second case, you are relying not as much on the writer's name as on what is written. Still, the person should merit respect. An immediate supervisor at work or a college teaching assistant is not worth troubling; ideal would be a corporate vice president or a tenured business professor. The recommendation should be as enthusiastic as if you had written it yourself—and that, effectively, is what you must do.

This type of letter is a mutual effort. Your job does not end once you've found someone to write it. You should be able to provide the author with an outline of what you want said, and you should have the opportunity to edit the essay yourself. What this means, basically, is that the author has to be a friend, someone who considers helping you out to be more important than being truly objective. An unemphatic recommendation from an unrenowned person will not do you any good.

If you find yourself writing a recommendation outline, you must determine what your prospective employers consider important. Your instinct is probably correct here, and chapter 4 offers more information on this subject. A professor can assess your abilities and accomplishments, but a past employer should concentrate on your job performance. The ideal letter contains only one or two general paragraphs, followed by three or four that discuss your job-related skills. It should not be over one and one-half pages long.

The Cover Letter

If there is a Catch-22 situation in job hunting, it involves the cover letter. Even in situations where it is not requested, such as in placing your résumé in a corporation's folder at your career center, you should attach a cover letter to your résumé. However, a review of the cover letter is one of the most common methods by which candidates are eliminated from the process. The cover letter is rarely anything but a liability, yet you must include it because its absence is worse.

The key to surviving a cover letter review is to keep it simple and take no chances. Don't think that a fancy or unusual one will disguise a weak résumé. I have never seen a cover letter help an otherwise unqualified application; all you can achieve by being unorthodox is to disqualify yourself.

There is a standard, accepted format for a cover letter. Diverge from it at your own risk:

> One sentence stating who you are and that you are looking for a job in the firm's industry. One sentence saying that you would like to apply for a position at the firm.
>
> Two or three sentences summarizing your qualifications for the job. No more.
>
> One or two sentences stating that a résumé is enclosed, and that you would like an interview. One sentence, if necessary, arranging the mechanics of getting back in touch. A final sentence stating your appreciation for their consideration and that you are awaiting a reply.

The most important concept to keep in mind when writing a

cover letter is that you are writing a cover letter. The worst are those that forget their purpose and instead dissolve into self-serving statements of qualifications. Some letters don't even include a request for a reply.

There are very few cover letter DOs. They are as follows:

- Know specifically what position you are applying for and what it entails.
- Know how to spell names. If you do not know to whom to write, a few well-placed phone calls are acceptable. (See "Walk-ons" for more information.)
- Use the same stationery for the cover letter and the résumé. Do not use gray paper or any other shade that photocopies poorly—most reviewers look at copies, not originals.
- Type single-spaced in proper business-letter form.

There are an infinite number of DON'Ts when it comes to cover letters. Here are a few of the most offensive:

- Unsubstantiated boasting. Don't say, "I expertly led swimming lessons," when you can say, "I directed swimming lessons for two-hundred children."
- Patronizing your reviewer with sentences like, "The management consulting business has become increasingly competitive, allowing only the most talented people to qualify and succeed."
- Starting your letter with, "My name is . . . ."
- Fancy language, exclamation points, or overdone signatures.
- Obvious (not word-processed) form letters. I couldn't believe some of the fill-in-the-blank letters I received. (They went straight into the trash.)
- Personalized letterhead. You are (or recently were) a student, not a corporate vice president. Likewise, printing up

and sending along business cards is a big mistake. This is an acceptable course of action only if you now hold a job that you think will be especially helpful in landing you a new one—and you don't mind getting telephone calls at the office.

- Two-page letters. Even five paragraphs is an excessive length.

You cannot be overly careful with a cover letter. As a little experiment, I spent fifteen minutes going through fifty cover letters from students at good schools, and found more than fifty bad sentences. Some blunders were due to what was said, others due to how it was said, and still others were due to both. Here are a few sorry examples:

"Let me tell you about myself."

"My interest in banking developed during my dad's tenure at General Motors."

"We are still awaiting impatiently to learn of our national ranking."

"A recent association was retained as a business assistant with a small venture capital firm."

"In addition and as the marketplace becomes increasingly international, I feel that it would be important to point out that I have travelled in both Eastern and Western Europe."

"I have worked for summers for the Apex Chemical Company, utilizing my analytical skills gain through my engineering education."

"My résumé may state that I am looking for a position in publishing, but I am also interested in banking."

"Thusly, I became a bouncer."

These sentences are by no means the worst that I have come across, and the fact that they were all found in a pile of fifty cover letters serves as an indication of how common such errors are. Keep it simple, keep it safe, and have an English major read your letter before you send it. A sample cover letter is shown on the following page.

Sample Cover Letter

                              Ivan T. Job
                              Box 1000, Joe College
                              Joestown, MA 12345
                              (413) 555-1234
                              January 1, 1990

Mr. Nate Likely
The BigBank Corporation
1 Wall Street
New York, NY 10001

Dear Mr. Likely:

  I am a senior majoring in economics at
Joe College, and I would like to obtain a
position in the investment banking industry
upon graduation. I am writing to apply for
a place in BigBank's Analyst Program in
Corporate Finance.

  I believe that my academic, extracurricular, and professional experience qualify me
for a position with your firm. Combined
with my interest in finance and my desire
to excel, this experience would allow me to
make a strong contribution to BigBank.

  My résumé is enclosed. I would like very
much to interview with BigBank when you
visit the Joe College campus in February.
Thank you for your time and consideration,
and I look forward to hearing from you.

                              Sincerely,

                              Ivan T. Job

                              Ivan T. Job

[Note: Recent graduates should change the first sentence accordingly. All walk-ons should replace the second-to-last sentence with something like: "At your convenience, I would appreciate the opportunity to interview with BigBank at your New York office." If you are not applying during the regular hiring season, you should mention that you will call them within several weeks to check on your status. Whether or not you are a walk-on, receiving no response after three weeks warrants a polite phone call.]

If You Don't Get an Interview

This is when the fun starts because you have nothing—or almost nothing—to lose. Within the limits of propriety, you can try any trick you like. For example, if you are denied an on-campus interview, send in another résumé with a cover letter indicating that you would like to interview at the firm's offices. If you make no reference to your on-campus denial, you may be accidentally grouped with the walk-on candidates and reviewed again. If your school is a prestigious one, you stand a better chance against the walk-ons.

Although things may seem pretty bleak if you are a true walk-on who has been rejected, don't give up. Try re-submitting your résumé through a different, more senior member of the firm. Paperwork control is so haphazard at some companies that a résumé can be reviewed three or four times before anyone realizes that he has seen it before.

It is important to stay within the limits of propriety because recruiters at different firms are often in communication. When I was a recruiting coordinator, my roommate had the same job at another investment bank, and we would regularly discuss unusual candidates. You can rest assured that my roommate heard all about the rejected candidate who, when requesting a second chance, called his denial a "sad misunderstanding." Anything crazy you do is likely to get around.

Once you have tried all the tricks you are comfortable with, there is one last thing you can do. Call the person who signed the rejection letter and let him know that:

1. You're sorry to bother him.
2. You were not granted an interview.
3. Your interest in the firm is still great.
4. You will be available should any openings come up.

While this approach rarely produces any results, it can't hurt if you do it politely. It is most likely to be helpful toward the end of the recruiting season, when some firms discover that they have not met their hiring quotas. Under those circumstances, a humble phone call—or letter, for that matter—can get you in the door.

The Campus Lottery

Most companies prefer, through the résumé-review process, to choose all the candidates whom they are going to interview. Nonetheless, many schools have some sort of lottery system in place through which on-campus interviews are doled out to students independent of the firm's judgment. While quite a few colleges, especially the larger ones, allow the firm to pick its entire interviewing schedule, some schools insist that the lottery be employed for as much as 100 percent of the interviews conducted on campus.

Originally put in place to round up candidates for those companies that didn't screen résumés, lottery systems are now hung onto desperately by guidance counselors who believe that students with unqualified résumés still deserve interviews. They may be too idealistic, but these counselors are correct in suggesting that résumé quality may have little relation to job performance. Unfortunately, most recruiters don't see it this way, and a bad résumé is almost guaranteed to bring you down before the job offer arrives (especially since your résumé is studied before every interview you enter). Nonetheless, a significant number of offers are initiated by the lottery interview.

Thus, if you are currently a senior, it can't hurt to use your school's lottery for all it's worth (and while it is unlikely, recent graduates should find out whether they are eligible for the lottery at their alma mater). These systems vary from school to school, and are often quite complicated, so make sure that you understand yours fully before submitting your interview requests.

If the system is at all flawed (many are), you can often slip between the cracks into or out of an interview, so keep on your toes. Stay on the good side of your guidance counselor, and you may be surprised at what turns up.

As the name implies, lottery systems are random; don't count on them alone to get you an interview. Send your résumé and cover letter to every firm that interests you, even if you are guaranteed a spot on the lottery schedule. When I conducted lottery interviews, I resented having to spend half an hour with someone whose résumé I had already rejected. But I respected those candidates more than the ones who arrived in my office having never before expressed an interest.

Form Letters

I remember the hours I spent as a college senior, poring over the letters I received from firms, studying every word for some hidden meaning, some indication that my interviewers had liked me just a little more or a little less than the other candidates. I knew that these companies were in the habit of using form letters, but some of the mail I was sent seemed so personal and sincere that it could hardly have been sent to anyone else. I remember one letter I received, after declining a callback interview at a Boston consulting firm, in which I was lauded as a "truly remarkable person"—this after only a thirty-minute Q & A blitz at a career fair. Boy, was I pleased with myself. Only slowly did I realize that I was about as remarkable as the rest of that firm's afternoon mail.

Form letters are used *whenever possible*. Unless you have tremendous cause to suspect otherwise, you can be relatively certain that any mail you get is a product of word-processing, and perhaps has even been approved by a committee. Don't waste your time trying to glean additional information from between the lines, and don't think that an enthusiastic letter means that you've made a friend for life. If an interviewer has something truly personal to say, he'll put it in a handwritten note.

3

Interview Preparation

Easier Than You Think

Preparing for a first-round interview, if done efficiently, is not a big job. The key to efficiency is knowing where to look. Don't waste your time, as so many do, digging up information that will be of no use to you during the interview. A *read-everything-I-can-get-my-hands-on* approach will jumble your head with so much useless data that you'll probably forget the job description.

The most effective methods of preparation involve people as the primary resource. Information interviews, though they may require a little extra work to set up, give you almost everything you need to know in half an hour's time. Company-sponsored information sessions, which you should think of as mandatory, spoon-feed you details about the job that you may not be able to find anywhere else. Both of these sources also provide you with the opportunity to make some friends in high places.

When doing your research, think about how you are going to use the information you collect. Nine times out of ten, the information comes in handy in only two places: answering questions intended to test your interest in the job (see chapter 4, section 9), and asking pertinent questions at the end of the interview. Once you feel truly prepared to handle those two tasks, you can probably stop your research.

Information Interviewing

An incredible resource that most college seniors and many recent graduates tend to neglect is the information interview. If you're creative and intelligent in how you seek and use them, information interviews can both give you the edge in your job interviews and provide access to corporations that are otherwise impenetrable.

Information interviews are by far the most helpful source of information for whatever industry you hope to enter. Not only do they give you the basic facts that you need in order to sound knowledgeable about the profession; they also relate these facts orally, in the way that people ordinarily discuss them. After one or two information interviews, you will have already determined what is considered important by people in the industry, as well as how to articulate it. By the time the real interviews come along, your reviewers will think that you've already spent a year in the industry.

Information interviews are also useful in overcoming the fits of nervousness that may accompany your first interview situations. Since no one is drilling you with questions, you can relax and get accustomed to the corporate environment at a calmer pace. They also give you a chance to smooth out the rough edges before the really important interviewing starts. But beware: If you hope to eventually land a job at the same firm, a faux pas during an information interview can be just as deadly as during the real thing. While it is not the purpose of the interview, *you are constantly being judged.*

Happily, this works both ways, and that's the main beauty of an information interview. If the person with whom you're talking takes a liking to you, you could very well end up with a *job* interview at the same firm. Professionals who conduct information interviews are often of fairly senior rank; if you impress them, there's a lot they can do about it. Always bring your résumé along to these meetings. Don't take it out of your folder—except under the pretense of seeking advice—but be ready to leave it with an interviewer who takes the bait. Because they offer you an alternative route to the pile-per-school résumé contest, information interviews are a particularly attractive alternative for walk-on candidates.

Even if you believe that you can conduct a successful job search simply by using your campus placement office (probably not a good idea), you will quickly find that a number of attractive firms do not visit your campus. You can try to access these firms through a résumé and cover letter, as already discussed in chapter 2, but first *try to get an information interview.* There will be plenty of time to throw yourself into the résumé pile later, if the need still exists.

Of course, getting an information interview isn't always easy. Start by networking through people you know (see *"Connections,"* chapter 2). If you have no connections at all, it is best to approach the firm through something other than its standard hiring function. Contact the company through its public relations or community affairs division, if one exists, and introduce yourself as someone studying the industry. If you're still in school, make sure that's obvious. At no time should you bring up your desire to work for the firm, because the moment you are declared a "candidate" you lose any advantage you had over the competition.

Some firms simply do not conduct information interviews, but don't give up until you're certain that this is the case. Even if it's just for the information, you should have at least one information interview in each industry that you are considering, *before the real interviews start.* If you can't get one, try to speak on the phone to someone you know in the field—a recent gradu-ate, for example. He may not be able to pull any strings for you, but he can definitely give you some valuable insight into the profession.

Information Interview Questions

You should already have a lot of questions in mind for your information interviews. While you are truly free to talk about whatever seems appropriate, the examples here will give you a good idea of what is generally acceptable.

What questions you ask and how you ask them depend, of course, on your relationship with the interviewer. The questions that follow would be appropriate for professionals whom you've never met before, but you needn't be so formal with people you already know. Don't turn off an old school chum or teammate by treating him like an anonymous counselor. Certain people like you enough to do you favors; to put aside your friendship in the name of corporate formality could alienate them.

Information interview questions can be split into three types: a) those that are appropriate if you have an upcoming interview in the same industry or at the same company; b) questions to ask if you do not yet have any interviews scheduled; and c) questions that are always acceptable.

Upcoming Interview

Now is a good time to prepare yourself for certain questions you may be asked during the interview by asking them yourself. You should generally use your questions to develop a better understanding of the company, the job, and what it takes to get the job. For example:

"How would you describe the role of your division? What, exactly, does it do?"

"What do you see as the greatest problem concerning your industry right now?"

"Can you tell me the history of your company?"

"What are the typical responsibilities of an entry-level recruit within your division?"

"What are the qualities that you think are most desired in an entry-level recruit?"

No Interviews Yet

In this case, you are probably looking for general advice on where to get started, as well as a possible access route to the interviewer's company. Without being too obvious, let the guy know that you'd happily work for him:

"I'm looking for a job in business, in order to work hard and get some good experience. If you were me, where would you start?"

"Are there challenging entry-level jobs available in your industry, that you're aware of?"

"Will you give me some advice on my résumé?"

"Honestly, do you think that with my record I will have much success finding an entry-level, career-path job in this industry?"

"Do you know someone whom I could talk to in order to find out more about opportunities in this industry?"

Always Good

These questions are also acceptable during traditional job-on-the-line interviews:

"Tell me about your job. Would you recommend a long-term career in your field?"

"Is an MBA required nowadays for advancement in this industry?"

"Is this a good time for your industry? Do you expect more of the same?"

"What are your favorite and least favorite aspects of this business?"

Information Sessions

For both seniors and recent graduates, the information sessions that many firms hold on campus provide an excellent opportunity to get a head start in acquiring knowledge and making contacts.

As far as knowledge is concerned, attending the information session is not as much of an advantage as missing it is a distinct disadvantage. Most candidates who interview will have attended the information session; if you do not, you will be conspicuous in two ways. First, you will seem less interested in the position. Many interviewers will ask, or discern, whether or not you attended their presentation. If you did not, and don't have a good excuse, you can only come off as uninterested or disorganized. (If you are a recent graduate and were still able to make it to the information session, they will be quite impressed.)

Second, you will be noticeably less prepared, both in terms of your understanding of the job and your knowledge of how to impress the interviewer. Quite a few presentations include descriptions of the firm's ideal candidate, and one or two companies even hand out a list of desired qualities, much like the one described in chapter 4. If information is power, ignorance of the idiosyncrasies of the employer's criteria can make you a weaker candidate.

Making contacts at information sessions is an art in itself. Most people don't try, and some try too hard, but few get it right. These contacts can be incredibly valuable: Those people giving campus presentations are often heavily involved in the interviewing process, and many are on the actual decision-making committees. At the time of the presentation, these people are most concerned about the year's harvest and will be at their warmest when it comes to appreciating your attention. Furthermore, since it is early in the season, they are not yet sick of the whole recruiting scene, and will view your interest with less jaded eyes.

Friends are made one-on-one, not in crowds, so the time to ask your questions is *after* the session, when everyone is mingling about. Questions asked during the group Q & A period rarely make the questioner look good. Leave those to somebody else, unless the Q & A period consists of an embarrassing silence—you'll be considered a hero for breaking the ice.

A question asked in a group, as most people seem to forget, should apply to practically everyone in the group. It should also address a subject that was at least briefly mentioned during the presentation. Avoid self-serving, show-offy, nerdy questions such as, "Your P/E Ratio went up eight percentage points this year. Would you credit this to marketing or R & D?" (And if you were actually considering that type of question, may I suggest graduate school?) Q & A questions should be asked in a casual, relaxed voice, but be devoid of any *likes* and *y'knows*. They should not sound as if they were prepared beforehand.

Although it may seem otherwise, the presentation team is visiting your school to talk about jobs, not about their firm, and this distinction applies equally to the questions you ask one-on-one after the session. Be interested in the industry as a place to work and about the mechanics of the specific job they are pushing. If anyone on the presentation team holds the job you are seeking, ask him to describe some of his experiences. Show an interest in a specific sector of the industry (one of the firm's product groups, for example), and if you are lucky they will offer to send you some information on it. This is the perfect *in*.

As in an information interview, one mention of your desire

for a job or a job interview will blow your cover. To bring your résumé is also a grave mistake. One final point: As helpful as these contacts can be, never resort to pushiness to get a recruiter's ear. Your ultimate goal here is to make an important friend or two, so a rushed or unpleasant conversation is worse than none at all.

Written Material

Your research of written material can be extremely quick. To be adequately informed you need only read the company's latest annual report, along with one general review such as *The Value Line* (available in most libraries). In the annual report, concern yourself only with text; you are not supposed to understand the financial statements.

Otherwise, you are responsible only for the information that the company sends you personally or provides at your career center library. If you have a campus interview scheduled with a firm that has neglected to provide the library with any written material about the job, there is nothing wrong with calling up the person who granted you the interview and asking if there is any information that he could send you. Offer to place a folder in the library for him. (If he says no, apologize for bothering him and tell him you'll do some more research on your own.)

If you have a walk-on interview scheduled, it is more than acceptable to call the firm and ask for some preparatory information. If you can't get in touch with your résumé-reviewer, you should always be able to get the public relations department to send you something general. If you don't have access to a business library, public relations will also be able to mail you an annual report.

You should also be aware of whether the company has been in the news lately. The only newspaper that everyone in business seems to care about is the *Wall Street Journal*, so that's all you need to read. Starting a few weeks before your interviews, skim it daily. While you don't want to bring it up during the interview, you should certainly be aware of any serious problems plaguing your prospective employer.

Before reading anything else, ask yourself if it is likely to contain information that you can actually put to use during the interview. Since most of the questions you ask and receive will address the company *as it relates to you,* you should put aside general information about the corporation until you have finished reading about the division of the firm that interests you and the job itself.

Performance Preparation

This is the side of interview preparation that most novice candidates neglect. Have you ever given a thirty-minute oral report with no index cards? That's what an interview is, yet many candidates think that research without rehearsal is enough. By the time the interview comes around, you want to have a good idea of what you are going to say *and* how you are going to say it. Not only should you have some prepared answers and questions (as discussed later), but you should be ready to state them articulately and convincingly.

But don't think of your interview as a recital; it's more like a jazz performance. Don't memorize your answers. Rather, memorize the *chords,* and you'll be able to *improvise* good answers. Practice your major statements once or twice—so that you know you can do it—and leave it at that.

I avoided interview workshops as a senior, but I now believe that they are a good idea. If your school provides them, go to one. Who knows, you may have some horrible subconscious twitch that only shows itself in interview situations. Ask the instructor if you have any problems.

Finally, prepare yourself emotionally. Visualize yourself having successful interviews. The best part of being prepared is feeling prepared, and the work that you have done should allow you to approach your interviews feeling confident and relaxed.

4

The First-Round Interview

Giving Them What They Want

The first-round interview—any interview, for that matter—is a faulty process, but it's the only one out there. Conducted at schools, career fairs, or on-site at the firm, most first-round interviews last twenty-five minutes and are either one-on-one or two-on-one. The average interviewer prefers conducting one-on-ones because they allow him, free from all scrutiny, to ask whatever ridiculous questions he desires. For that reason, you shouldn't worry about two-on-ones: You may feel ganged up on, but the questions will probably be easier and more predictable.

Generally speaking, the goal of every first-round interviewer is the same: to determine, as efficiently as possible, which candidates are likely to receive an offer when brought back for a full day of interviews. Therefore, because each callback interviewer may be looking for a different thing, the first-round interviewer, in anticipation, must try to cover *every*thing. (A common diversion at my firm was to give an especially hard time to interviewers whose candidates struck out in the callbacks—particularly if those candidates were recruited from the interviewers' alma maters. As a result, our first-round interviewers tended to be fairly conservative and as thorough as possible. They were much more likely to bring back solid, all-around candidates than idiosyncratic geniuses.) As you will see, the very nature of the interviewing process demands that your talents be distributed evenly across a wide variety of categories.

Statistically, the first-round interview is much less of a challenge than the résumé-screen. The fact is that I would enter prescreened interviews wanting to hire everyone I met—almost everyone was qualified. The candidates then went on to disqualify themselves, and they usually did so due to one of three things:

1. personality problems;
2. interviewing problems; or
3. ignorance of what I was looking for in a candidate.

Personality problems are addressed at the end of this chapter, but a lot of them, unfortunately, are hard to control. Trust me when I tell you that some people just aren't cut out for business. *Interviewing problems,* such as nervousness and improper etiquette, are more easily overcome and are discussed throughout this chapter and the next. *Knowing specifically what qualities the interviewer is looking for,* the ultimate key to your success, is the main topic of the pages that follow.

What the Interviewer Is Looking For

I used to pride myself on being an effective interviewer, but in retrospect I'm not so sure that I did a very good job (or that anyone does, for that matter). It is true that most recruiters go into interviews knowing exactly what they want from a candidate, but only a few know how to go about getting it. Each interviewer has his favorite questions, designed to discern a dozen or so hidden facts about the applicant. But most, as hard as they try, stop short of asking all the questions necessary to get the complete picture. Your job, as interviewee, is not just to perform well in the categories the recruiter is able to cover *but also to provide the desired responses to the questions he forgets to ask.*

This task becomes much easier when you realize that almost every interviewer, in talking with you, is trying to fill out a sheet. This sheet is one or two pages long and lists between five and ten categories in which you are to be rated. Spaces are usually provided beside each category for evidence and commentary. A *final recommendation* space at the end is intended to take all of the categories into account.

When an interviewer does a less-than-perfect job, as is usually the case, he is left at the end of the interview writing down guessed-at answers for as many as half of the categories on his sheet. When a qualified candidate does a less-than-adequate job, it is often because his answers are not designed to receive good marks. If you know what topics are on the sheet, however, you can both direct your responses to them, and help the interviewer to complete *every* category in your favor.

If I had been a completely up-front, no-bull type of interviewer, I suppose that I would have placed the sheet in front of each candidate and had the two of us go through it together. I never did that, of course, and I doubt that any recruiter ever will. The best you can do is to guess, based on the information I am about to provide, what topics are being investigated and then subtly find a way to address them all during the interview.

This approach is necessary because most selection committees consist of people who review sheets, not people who discuss people. This is especially true when it comes to the callback interviews, when your fate may be determined by a group of four or five people, only one or two of whom have actually interviewed you. All they have to go on are the rating sheets that they have collected. Even in the case of the first-round interview, your face will soon be forgotten, and all that will remain is the sheet.

Fortunately, there is a great deal of similarity in what most firms are looking for in an entry-level hire, which means that these sheets all look pretty much the same. I have divided the topics usually covered into ten categories. While some firms may not address every category, most should address the majority of them:

1. intelligence and analytical ability
2. creativity and flexibility
3. communication skills
4. work experience and required technical skills
5. leadership qualities/team-playing ability
6. initiative and entrepreneurship
7. energy and stamina
8. maturity
9. interest in the position
10. personal qualities and personality

The next ten sections discuss each category independently, focusing on what exactly is desired and how to come across in the correct way. Also provided are some typical questions interviewers ask in order to reach conclusions regarding your qualifications in each category. Read each section with a dual purpose in mind: to prepare yourself for questions in that category, and to prepare yourself to perform well even in those categories that the interviewer neglects to investigate.

1. Intelligence and Analytical Ability

More than most other categories, this one should be well addressed by your résumé. If not, consider yourself lucky to have gotten an interview in the first place. By *intelligence*, I mean raw intelligence, as documented by high test scores, good grades, and other academic achievements. Otherwise, intelligence is difficult to quantify, but somehow we interviewers find it easy to jump to conclusions. *Analytical ability*, like intelligence, is also manifested in test scores (Math SAT, GMAT) and grades (math and science classes), but in addition most interviewers have a number of questions at their disposal to test your quantitative problem-solving ability.

In interviewing candidates, I found that analytical ability was less often a skill than a state of mind. Do you enjoy solving problems? Do you like computers, mind-benders, and cross-word puzzles? Most importantly, when presented with an analytical challenge, do you take the time to define the parameters, understand the goal, and then work step-by-step to a conclusion? Recruiters ask analytical questions not just to get an answer but to see how your mind works. It is your thought process that will tell them whether you are analytical or not.

Before you are asked any tricky questions, make sure you have provided your interviewer with whatever evidence you can muster—hopefully, a lot of it is on your résumé. When I knew that a candidate had a GMAT score of 700, he was usually spared the really tough ones; instead, I would spend my time investigating the categories that were still uncertain. A high GPA, however, was rarely convincing unless it came from a top-notch school—I interviewed far too many non-analytical computer science 4.0s to let those grades go unchallenged.

Two types of questions test analytical ability. The first type allows you to tell them that you are analytical; the second type makes you prove it. The first four questions below, all common, make it easy for you to come across as an analytical, intelligent person. You need only remember that your analytical ability is what they have in mind. The final three questions, however, test this ability outright. This type of question varies in difficulty but always requires, more than anything else, a cool head and a desire to think analytically. If it has one obvious solution (based on math, not instinct), then you needn't walk the interviewer through your problem-solving process. But if the answer is less certain—or you are less certain of it—then you should work it out aloud, step-by-step.

Type One

Question: **What were your best and worst courses in college?**

Answer/Explanation: You may have done well in all different types of courses, and you can certainly say so. But when choosing one or two courses to name as best, don't waste your time on Shakespeare or Music 101. Mention a physics course, a computer course—something that just reeks of analytical thinking. As far as *worst* goes, that's a no-win situation. Of the courses in which you did badly, if any, mention one that has nothing to do with math or science or the job in question—the more obscure, the better. Extenuating circumstances such as illness or insane professors also deserve mention if they played a role.

Q: **What were your favorite and least favorite courses in college?**

A/E: This question also tests *personality* and *interest.* If your favorite course sounds boring, so do you; if it has nothing to do with the job, you may seem uninterested. Your favorite course need not be analytical—the big mistake would be to name an analytical course as your *least* favorite.

Q: **Would you describe yourself as more analytical or verbal?**

A/E: Although it sounds rather transparent, this question is asked by many interviewers largely because many interviewees don't think to tailor their answers to the job requirements (and they're too honest). The ideal candidate for most entry-level jobs is someone analytical by nature who happens to have excellent reading and writing skills. You'll notice how that definition doesn't really answer the question, and neither should your response.

This question is actually a trick to get you to betray a lack of either analytical or verbal skills. Although most jobs tax one side of the brain over the other, the only way to come off a winner is to demonstrate strength in both areas. Thus, your answer should take the form of either, "It's hard to say, because...," or "Analytical, but...." In both cases it is essential that you provide positive evidence supporting your conclusion.

Q: **Why aren't your grades higher?**

A/E: If your grades are low, you are lucky to receive this question, because it gives you a chance to disassociate your grades from the criteria that are used to rate your intelligence. When I thought that candidates' grades were too low for a hire, I would tell them straight out, in hopes of hearing some justification. Most candidates blurted out wimpy excuses, which got them nowhere. Only one or two candidates exercised a different approach that truly impressed me. It went something like this:

> "Well, I guess some people go to college to get good grades, but that just wasn't what I was there for. I financed half of my tuition by working during summers and during the school year, and if you think I was going to spend all of my money on gut courses, you must be crazy (*smile*). My goal was to take the courses that would improve me the most, not test some knowledge I had already accumulated in high school, etc., etc. . . . . ."

This response is effective because it turns the question into one about *motivation* rather than intelligence. It makes you look mature and directed, and it makes the interviewer believe, at least temporarily, that grades aren't all that important after all. The candidate who gave me that response had a C+ average— a full point below almost everyone else we interviewed—yet she ended up with the job.

Another motivation-oriented approach begins with the same initial sentence as the one above, followed by a description of how you put most of your energy into extracurricular activities. Since employment involves no extracurricular activities, you will be able to focus 100 percent of your attention on the job. Once again, your intelligence is removed from the discussion.

Type Two

Q: **You have two hours to drive to a meeting, and you must average fifty miles per hour to get there on time. The first half of your trip, distance-wise, is uphill, and the second half is downhill. If you get to the top of the hill having averaged twenty miles per hour, how fast must you drive downhill to avoid being late?**

A/E: You're already late (think about it). The candidates who get this type of question wrong are either too nervous to think clearly or too aggressive to sit through a moment of silence before they start to talk. If you find yourself rushing to answer, you would be wise to first sit back and begin the solution on a hypothetical piece of paper in your head.

Q: **You have a cup of coffee that is piping hot and an ounce of cream at room temperature. You want the coffee to be as cold as possible in three minutes. Do you add the cream immediately, or do you wait until the end of the three minutes to add it?**

A/E: I used to love asking this one, as hundreds of my hapless victims would attest. At the time, I wasn't even sure of the correct answer; I only wanted to see the candidate's thought process in action. Most candidates answered the question incorrectly, but only half of them ended up disappointing me by avoiding analytical thought. Their deficient responses included the following:

"I would add the cream right away, because it's cold, and I want the coffee to get cold."

"I would wait for the end because the coffee will be coldest right after I shock it with the cream."

"I don't like coffee." (Actually a pretty good answer, but the candidate then continued to avoid the question.)

"Well, I guess I'd add a tiny bit of cream, and then stir it with a spoon, and then blow on it a bit, add some more cream, taste it . . . ." (No kidding.)

An acceptable response would be:

"It doesn't matter, because you have a system with a set amount of energy. The coffee has x calories, and the cream has y calories. Apart or together, that energy should dissipate at the same rate."

That answer is actually incorrect, but it's impressive. The right answer, supposedly, is that you add the cream at the end, because an object's cooling speed is proportional to the difference between its temperature and room temperature. You would probably have to be a chemistry major to come up with that response, but no big deal—the candidate who said, "It doesn't matter," and talked in calories still got the offer.

A word of warning: Some candidates, for the sake of conversation, would present me with various brain-teasers they had heard. This practice may seem perfectly harmless, but it wasn't. I would get so annoyed at not being able to solve one of these questions, that I could never again think of the candidate in a positive light.

Q: **Mathematically speaking, what are your chances of getting this job? Don't ask me any questions, but let me know the assumptions that you are making.**

A/E: This question also offers an opportunity to show your personality and self-confidence, but don't let that get in the way of performing the simple math that the interviewer wants to see exhibited. An acceptable answer would be:

"Well, I would like to think that, since this is the job that I feel best suited for, my chances are better than most of the people you'll be interviewing today. But I know there's quite a bit of competition, so for the sake of argument I'll assume that everyone you interview automatically has the same likelihood of being hired. You are interviewing 2 schedules of 12 candidates at this school, which makes 24. I'll assume you visit 10 schools, so that's 240, plus, say, 40 walk-ons makes 280. You mentioned that you are filling 10 positions, so you'll probably have to make 20 offers. Twenty out of 280 is one-fourteenth, or about 7 percent."

Nervousness

There is nothing wrong with being nervous about an interview. As a college senior I got uptight about almost every interview I had, and even as an interviewer I would sometimes feel fidgety. Whatever side of the desk you find yourself on, an interview situation requires you to play a role, so a bit of stage fright is to be expected.

Letting your nervousness show, however, is a lethal mistake. Like most of my colleagues, I simply would not allow myself to hire an excessively nervous candidate. Why? Because if you're scared stiff during an interview, you'll be equally petrified in a client meeting, and beyond help if you have to make any sort of independent presentation. Frankly, if the thought of interviewing makes your forehead bead with sweat, you probably don't belong in the business world at all.

But there are steps that you can take to keep your nervousness under cover. The most effective are well known: rehearsing your responses, picturing your interviewers in their underwear, etc. . . .; these can all be helpful. To them I would add: interviewing absolutely as much as possible—even for jobs you don't really want—

and repeatedly "previsualizing" yourself as feeling comfortable during the interview. Also, I find that a handkerchief or a piece of tissue in a right-hand pocket can take care of that sweaty palm. Whatever steps you have to take, take them, because if you're going to look tremendously nervous, you may as well not even show up.

Perhaps things might seem a bit easier if you realize that, yes, you are being judged, but your interviewers recognize that they are being judged as well. Recruiters are almost equally absorbed by their desire to impress; when an interviewer gets dressed in the morning, he chooses his clothes with you in mind. He can't help but feel a bit self-conscious at the prospect of being the sole representative of an entire corporation. More than that, he is nervous about simply making himself look good to you. Only the most seasoned career interviewer doesn't share your feelings of vulnerability. So you can take some comfort in the fact that you are not alone, and that your position of emotional disadvantage is not absolute.

2. Creativity and Flexibility

A creative, flexible person is able to approach problems in new and unusual ways. He does not fear the status quo, but is always looking for a way to make things better. As you might expect, this quality has become increasingly valuable in recent years, even among entry-level recruits. A number of questions test this quality, but you can also score high based strictly on what you do and who you are. Do you paint, play jazz guitar, or write short stories? Don't hide it. Nor should you set aside your sense of humor—often that's all the interviewer has to go on.

You don't want to come off as outrageous or bizarre, but you must do something to distinguish yourself in this department. Judging from the behavior of most of the people I've interviewed, especially business majors, very few candidates realize that this category exists. For the sake of our country's future, I hope that they were modestly hiding their creativity from me. More than any other box on my review sheet, I would have to check off *fair* in this category for want of any real evidence.

Most questions in this area focus more strongly on flexibility than creativity. They require you to take a step back, fully assess your resources, and then accomplish something that you've never been taught how to do. Others make you think about the things you've always taken for granted. Some rare questions, like the last one that follows, test the limits of your imagination.

Q: **You're at work and I ask you to find out approximately how many gas stations there are in the United States. How would you go about doing it?**

A/E: Your guess is as good as mine on this one, but most good solutions would involve determining the answer for a microcosm, such as a typical town, and expanding it to cover the entire country. Before doing so, however, mention that you could do two things: First, consult someone in the industry, such as a public relations representative at Mobil, and ask him for any advice on how to go about the problem. Second, in hope that the answer may already be recorded, give the U. S. Census Bureau a try. These steps evoke two powerful rules for working efficiently: Bring in an expert, and don't do anything that has already been done for you.

If neither of these attempts were to bear fruit, you should probably call back your friend at Mobil and ask him: a) how many Mobil stations there are; and b) what percentage of the country's gasoline Mobil sells (or just ask for a volume figure and then call the Census Bureau for national fuel consumption). From that point on it's simple math to get an answer.

Q: **Why are manhole covers round?**

A/E: This is an all-time favorite, with many correct answers:

1. Because a round object cannot fall down a similarly shaped hole of the same size, while a square or any other shape can. (Try it some time.)
2. Because you can roll a round object on its edge. Square manhole covers would be much more difficult to move.
3. No matter how you rotate it, it still fits in the hole.
4. Because round objects distribute stress evenly. (That is also a reason why manholes and waterpipes are tubular.)

Despite all of these possible solutions—and more, probably—I rarely found a candidate who could answer this question. My response as an undergraduate was, "Because manholes are round." Luckily, my interviewer was amused and let it slide. My advice for this type of question, in retrospect, is to picture the object in use and consider, step by step, how and why it works.

Q: **You can have dinner with anyone throughout history. Whom would you choose?**

A/E: This question tests how far you can expand your mind. You may want to impress your interviewer with an interest in business, but Henry Ford sounds pretty lame compared to Winston Churchill, who pales next to Julius Caesar. What about Queen Elizabeth I, Gandhi, Karl Marx, or Plato? It is a truly impressive candidate who invites both Jesus and Buddha so that they can work out their differences. If you say Lee Iacocca or Donald Trump, please send me back this book. I don't know you.

3. Communication Skills

In both getting and keeping a job, this category is perhaps the most important. Communication skills cover the gamut from clear speaking to clear thinking and are manifested in almost everything you do. A great communicator, even devoid of other skills, can accomplish anything. (A few recent examples may come to mind.)

Sadly, there is not much that you can do at this point if your abilities are lacking. Years of faithful reading, writing, and public speaking can correct a serious communication difficulty, but in the short run you can probably only hope to make a superficial impact on the way you come across. Even a small improvement, however, can make all the difference in an interview situation.

This point makes sense in light of the fact that most interviewers base their judgment on how you sound rather than how you truly think. So many candidates have trouble spitting out grammatically correct, well-enunciated sentences, that those who do can't help but earn a good rating. Even in bridging the gap from *good* to *excellent*, it is more your vocabulary than your thought process that will make a difference.

So, without forgetting how to think, concentrate on the *surface*. First, eliminate any *likes* and *y'knows* from your vocabulary. If used frequently, they are simply not acceptable. Saying *um*, though not as bad, can also be a liability. A thoughtful silence is much more impressive. Slang words that haven't yet made it into the dictionary are a bad idea, and, just to be safe, don't curse either.

Regional accents are a difficult subject. While there may not be much that you can do about them, Boston, Brooklyn, and "Lon Giland" accents make you sound unsophisticated. Valley-girl accents—and the sister dialect to be found in certain parts of New Jersey—come off as flighty and overprivileged. To people from the north or west, a southern drawl sounds charming but uneducated. Unless you are interviewing locally, tone down your accent as much as possible without faking it. Only genuine British, French, and other highly romanticized foreign accents can be of any help. Otherwise, try to speak like the people on the "NBC Nightly News." If you tend to mumble or talk too quickly, you've probably gotten away with it until now, but it can't continue to run unchecked. If a recruiter can't understand what you're saying, he probably won't care enough to ask you to repeat it.

There are a number of questions that interviewers may ask to specifically test your communication skills, but these skills are obviously tested by every question you answer. If you have not done much interviewing, and especially if you are nervous, you may have difficulty being your normal, articulate self. One solution is to be prepared with ready answers to the questions that you know you will be asked. While too many prepared responses will make you sound insincere, a few can start the words flowing. Besides, the process of developing prepared answers occurs naturally as you are asked the same questions over and over. Why not give it a head start? Just make certain that you don't end up sounding like a tape recorder.

The following questions, directly or indirectly, give the interviewer a strong sense of your communication skills:

Q: **Tell me about your senior thesis (or another major term paper).**

A/E: This question is a good communication skills test because it asks you to describe something that you should know quite a bit about to someone who is not familiar with it. It may also force you to take a subject that is primarily technical in nature and put it into layman's terms. In addition, it probably requires that you condense some fairly complicated issues into relatively few words.

The keys to success in this endeavor are to accurately assess the knowledge of your interviewer and to remember that your time is limited. Underestimating the recruiter's intelligence will leave him insulted; overestimating it will leave him confused and insecure. It is perfectly acceptable to preface your response with a question such as, "Did you study much biology in school?" If you are still unsure of your audience, you are safe assuming a level of knowledge similar to that of your college roommates. Aside from their own business, people usually don't learn very much after college.

As you describe your paper, continually keep in mind that you only have a few minutes to tell the whole story. Decide, before it's too late, what level of detail your description cannot afford to go beyond. The most common error associated with this type of question is delving too deep and not resolving the discussion in a reasonable amount of time.

Q: Describe your responsibilities on your last job.

A/E: This question, which addresses work experience as well, brings the previous question's challenge into the sphere of business. Since much of doing a good job depends on understanding your assignments—and eventually giving clear ones yourself—interviewers want to know if you can intelligibly describe some of the assignments you've had.

Once again, heed the time and the interviewer's level of knowledge. As with the previous question, you will be better off if you enter the interview with some idea in your head of specifically what you are going to say. In your responses, inconspicuously mention the responsibilities of your last job that seem similar to those of the job in question.

Q: Read any good books lately?

A/E: Most articulate people are well read, and some interviewers esteem ongoing leisure-time reading as a hallmark of communication skills. Also, the ability to understand and succinctly describe something you've read is a required skill for most jobs, and for this reason many recruiters like to test it.

Remember that your personality is also being tested, so choose something that makes you sound interesting. Don't say *Money* magazine or *Businessweek* unless you enjoy the job hunt and want it to go on forever. *In Search of Excellence* or another book on business theory is only acceptable if you truly enjoyed it and can make that plain. Much better is something remotely business-related, if at all, that inspires an animated explanation. If the interviewer hasn't read it, then you've managed to sidestep the reading comprehension exam.

Since the recruiter is perhaps looking for a steady reading habit, you can quickly satisfy him by mentioning the book that you are "currently reading." Even if you choose to describe an old favorite, let him know that you're currently in the middle of something else.

4. Work Experience and Required Technical Skills

This is another category that your résumé should satisfy but that recruiters, quite reasonably, feel the need to confirm in person. Your old jobs that sounded so impressive when reduced to two sentences must now bear the weight of a more thorough investigation. Likewise, your "knowledge of Pascal" must be proven to refer to a computer language rather than a friend from Paris.

Preparation for questions in this area is simple. Using your résumé as a jumping-off point, mentally structure descriptions of your responsibilities at each job. After a brief overview, focus on one or two projects of specific interest. Stress the situations in which you worked independently, made significant decisions, or were able to gain additional responsibility. As in your résumé, shy away from the daily tedium.

Here are some employment-related questions that I would often ask:

Q: **Can you walk me through your résumé?**

A/E: (One candidate, as his response, lay his résumé at my feet and offered to help me out of my chair. *I* was amused, but I can't make any guarantees.) In one form or another, this question will be asked of you in every interview you have. If you go through the preparation exercise just described, you have nothing to worry about. Characterize each job as enjoyable and challenging, but not overly difficult.

Remember that you have nothing to gain by speaking poorly of your previous jobs. The worse you make the jobs look, the worse you look. Saying that a job was dull means that you're either hard to satisfy or too complacent to do anything about your own situation. Don't bring up any workplace personality conflicts. Even if they were "the other guy's fault," they can't help but reflect badly on you.

Q: **What specific skills did you develop on your last job that you would consider useful here?**

A/E: You should take this type of question in two different directions: specific technical skills and general job skills. Spend most of your time on the first and mention the second as the icing on the cake. If you are uncertain as to the exact nature of the technical jobs that you'll be performing, begin your answer with a question such as, "What sort of software packages do you typically use?" or "Can you tell me a little bit about your accounting methodology?" Once you know the answer, you'll be the candidate most likely to give them the response they are looking for.

Let's say a recruiter tells you that newly hired employees perform analyses with in-house software packages. Quickly rattle off all of the different software programs you've used and mention that you're accustomed to mastering new ones. If you've done some programming, suggest that you might be able to code some more software if they so desire. This comment will impress the older interviewers in particular. If your experience is severely limited, pick one analytical feat you've performed and go into detail on it. Never admit a deficiency unless asked straight out.

Once you've amazed them with your technical wizardry, mention that your work experiences have also taught you much that isn't technical in nature. There's a lot more to being successful at work than just getting the numbers right, such as working with secretaries, sticking to deadlines, and contributing to the positive atmosphere of an office. Let them know that you don't take these aspects of the job for granted.

Telephone Interviews

This practice has gotten such bad press that it will probably never become common, but don't be surprised if you come out of the shower one day to questions about your career plans. However unpleasant, telephone interviewing will persist for as long as it is cost effective, which may be forever. (Every time a recruiter has to spend half an hour locked in an office with a nerd, ten-minute telephone screens become more attractive.)

For college seniors, telephone interviews are most awkward because they are rarely received at opportune times. Even if you're not in the middle of a shaving-cream fight, chances are that your roommate is cranking the stereo. Whatever you do, don't try to participate in a telephone interview unless peace and quiet prevail. If you cannot lock everyone else out of the room, arrange a time to call the interviewer back. Do not attempt to hide your situation from the interviewer. You are a college student. If you share a phone and the dorm is in mayhem, he should understand your difficulty.

No matter what the situation, take the time to compose yourself before you talk. Also, keep your job-search paraphernalia in an easily accessible place; having your résumé in view can greatly enhance your performance. A calculator could also be helpful. (You never know what they might throw at you.)

5. Leadership Qualities/Team-Playing Ability

Are you a leader *and* a team player? One of the toughest challenges of interviewing will be convincing recruiters that you possess both of these mutually exclusive qualities. I remember failing at this task in at least two separate interviews. My failure, which could have been avoided, was due to my ignorance of this fact: A true team player will not easily let on that he is also a leader. Boasting, even if it's substantiated, is not a team-playing quality.

Thus, you are free to speak at length about your team-playing experience, but your leadership ability must speak for itself. Stress your positions of leadership on your résumé, but during the interview only mention them indirectly. "When I was working as features editor for the campus newspaper, I decided that I wanted to graduate into a job with as many writing responsibilities as possible," is much better than, "After only one year on the campus newspaper staff, I was named features editor."

Let your leadership qualities come across in an unspoken way. Don't bury your charisma: An enthusiastic smile says more about your leadership abilities than anything on your résumé. Charisma becomes especially important, of course, if you don't have any leadership experience to put on your résumé. Remember that, even in this case, you won't get anywhere trying to *convince* an interviewer that you are a leader.

Because this topic is so sensitive, the questions that you are likely to be asked are simple, but dangerous. Don't take a question at face value if answering it will make you compromise your modesty. For example:

Q: **We only hire "stars." Are you a "star"?**

A/E: This question, often followed by, "But then, are you a team player?" is a common trap. As just discussed, you won't get away with telling them flat out that you are a "star." If you see through to the purpose of the question, then you are 90 percent on your way to providing an acceptable answer. Without denying your stardom, work toward modesty in your response.

The perfect answer, to my mind, would sound something like this:

> "Well, I'd hesitate to use the word 'star' because it carries all sorts of negative connotations. For example, it usually isn't very easy to work with 'stars' because they are used to accomplishing things alone. But, if all you mean by 'star' is someone who has a record of high achievement, then I would like to think that I qualify."

Q: **What makes you better than everyone else I'm interviewing today?**

A/E: This question provides a similar trap. To escape it you must compliment yourself without bragging, which is almost impossible. But there is a way. Rather than talking about *who you are*, address such areas as *what you do* and *what you like*. The best answer I ever received made full use of this principle:

> "I certainly can't tell you that I'm the best candidate you'll see today, but I think that I may be the hardest worker. If I had to pick a certain quality that makes me special, it's probably that I enjoy working with all kinds of

people. That has been a major requirement of my other jobs, and it's something I'm very glad I've developed."

Q: **Tell me about your extracurricular activities.**

A/E: You should already know how to respond to this one; I've included it mainly because you'll receive it in almost every interview you enter. Its purpose is twofold: first, to investigate the leadership/team-playing issue; and second, to ascertain whether your extracurricular activity was more than superficial.

To satisfy the first count, talk enthusiastically about what your clubs and teams accomplished, using the word *we* rather than *I* wherever possible. Your individual feats will already be plainly stated by your résumé. To satisfy the second, let them know that a certain activity, "really took away from my study time, but I felt that it was worth it." As suggested in chapter 2, extracurricular activities serve both as a buffer for mediocre grades and as proof that you've kept yourself busy.

The Lottery Interview

As described in chapter 2, most schools' lottery systems are intended to partially override companies' résumé-screening procedures. Since these systems are totally random, you have no guarantee of receiving the interviews you want. But if you think that landing a lottery interview is a difficult task, just wait until you try to impress the interviewer. Making something of a lottery interview is no mean feat.

Despite the lower odds of getting a callback from a lottery interview, it's not impossible. Each year that I was involved in entry-level recruiting, we hired at least one candidate through the lottery system, and that was after having already denied that candidate's résumé in the original screen. Since, as interviewers, we were forced to sit through the lottery interviews, we also were determined to make something of them.

If you find yourself in a lottery interview after having been denied in the prescreen, your initial reaction may be the same as mine when I was once in that position: to spend the entire interview trying to convince the interviewer that you deserved to be selected. I had thought, "I know what they're looking for in a candidate, I know my qualifications, so I'll take them through their criteria, one by one, and show them that they were wrong." I entered the interview—with a Salomon Brothers' analyst—aggressive but cheerful, took control of the flow from the minute I sat down, and watched myself crash and burn.

My strategy, which seemed good at the time, was particularly inept for a number of reasons. First, in trying to control the interview, I was ignoring the fact that interviewers, especially young ones, have egos that need stroking. Second, in choosing to address the fact that I had not received a prescreen interview, I was reminding the interviewer both that he was forced to interview me against his will and that I was not one of the better candidates (at least not to him, and that's all that mattered). Third, and most stupidly, I was telling the interviewer that he had made a mistake. He had just met me, and I was already insulting him. Was he then supposed to give me a job?

The funniest thing is that the interviewer, until I entered his office, may have considered me a strong candidate anyway—I've already discussed how a good number of qualified résumés are tossed away simply due to the sheer volume of applicants. The wisest move would probably have been to ignore my disadvantaged status and pretend that I was going through a standard prescreen interview.

I would suggest the same strategy for you, but only if you are convinced that you are a top-quality candidate who was removed from the process by chance. How can you tell? If seven companies out of ten in a given industry grant you prescreen interviews, chances are that the other three were just bad luck. If the *only* interviews you receive are by lottery, get a clue: You're going to have to do something unusual during the interview to turn yourself into a qualified candidate. As an interviewer, there was little that I found more annoying than wasting my time with plainly undistinguished applicants who acted as if they had nothing to prove.

So, if you're fairly certain that you owe your interview only to luck, you have to prove your case without making the same mistakes that I did. If your résumé is well put together, your grades, activities, and/or work experience must be lacking. What compensating qualities, even intangible ones, do you have? Without taking control of the interview, try to make these plain. It also wouldn't hurt to provide evidence intended to allay the interviewer's fears regarding your intelligence and experience. Remember that you probably have nothing to lose in this case, so unconventional approaches are acceptable.

And no matter what, don't get your hopes up, because the odds are still slim. Since the résumé turns up repeatedly during the selection process, firms that have rejected it once will get the chance to reject it again. Those lottery candidates that my firm hired were not that far from landing prescreen interviews in the first place. If you're planning to use the lottery system as a means to interview over your head, you could be in for some trouble.

6. Initiative and Entrepreneurship

Are you prepared to take the ball and run with it? If I give you some rope, will you make knots or will you hang yourself with it? Are you HUNGRY? All of these questions, believe it or not, were thrown my way when I was applying for jobs. It was difficult enough translating them from recruiterspeak into English, and harder yet to respond with conviction. As is the case with most college seniors, my entrepreneurial experience was quite limited.

But, if you know where to dig, deeper investigation can unearth the initiative in all of us. Start with the first decision that you ever made for yourself, and work your way to the most recent time that you chose to work *outside the system*. Did you spend a semester abroad, conduct an independent study, or choose an interdisciplinary major? Did you spend a summer self-employed? There's really very little difference between mowing lawns for the neighbors and "starting a small landscaping company." These activities are worth mentioning in your interview.

The same paradox exists with *initiative and entrepreneurship* that exists with *leadership ability*. In the same way that many firms like to hire leaders and turn them into followers, so do they like to hire entrepreneurs and turn them into simple cogs in the corporate machinery. You must demonstrate initiative to qualify as one of the people they want, but you must keep it in check to qualify as one of the people they'll hire.

For their entry-level positions, companies look for hardworking self-starters who are ambitious yet know when to take no for an answer. If you seem too entrepreneurial in your business approach, your interviewers will have two fears: fear that you'll be after your boss's job and, more often, fear that you won't be happy as an assistant to an assistant. For that very reason we once had to turn down a candidate who, during college, had started a two-million-dollar corporation. We didn't know why he wanted the job we were selling, but we knew that he wouldn't want it for long.

So display your initiative without going overboard. Your main goal at this age is to work hard and make a contribution to a major corporation. "Movers and shakers" and "large-scale change agents" might be heavily recruited for upper-level management, but they aren't at your level.

Most questions in this category are more straightforward than the three mentioned at the outset. If you recognize when you hear them that your initiative and entrepreneurship are under investigation, then your responses will be more than adequate.

Q: **If you could change one thing about your college, what would it be?**

A/E: A common recruiter's gripe with the American educational system is that it cranks out thousands of identical graduates, each of whom has blindly followed the same prescribed path without ever thinking for himself. These people, who can find little worth changing in their schools, will usually lack the ability to initiate any improvement at the office.

Without condemning your college, think of some aspect of it that you could change for the better. Student–faculty relations and the housing system, for example, are much more appropriate topics than the number of whirlpools at the gym. Without being unrealistic, suggest a new system that you think would function more smoothly.

Q: **Describe one change you instituted at your last summer job.**

A/E: Be ready for this one because having no examples to cite can be embarrassing. Make a mental note of a procedure that you made more efficient, an unnecessary cost that you eliminated, or some other reform that you were responsible for, and be ready to discuss it. In no instances, however, should you mention or imply that you stepped on anybody's toes or that the change was not overwhelmingly favored.

Q: **Where do you see yourself in twenty years?**

A/E: Recruiters like this question because it provides a quick and accurate gauge of the applicant's ambition. The ideal candidate, without wanting instant autonomy, would probably harbor hopes of being self-employed by that age, perhaps in the same industry. At the same time, since a high premium is placed on loyalty, he wouldn't rule out the possibility of still being with the same company.

In fact, you can score instant points by bemoaning the general lack of employee loyalty that seems to have infected corporate America lately. Most interviewers have seen a good number of their prize recruits jump to other firms after six months on the job and are generally disgusted by the whole scene. Without making any promises, you might take the opportunity to let them know that job-hopping is not your style.

The worst answers, besides ignoring the concept of loyalty, betray either too much or too little ambition. It is hard to say which is worse: fully expecting to be CEO of General Motors or not wanting anything more out of life than the first job. Give either response and you're out of the running.

The Stress Interview

Rare, stupid, and often representative of the organization (or at least the job), the "stress interview" should make you think twice about accepting an offer from the firm that uses it. (You have to determine through other channels whether it's the job or just the interview that's a pain in the neck.) Unfortunately, there still exist certain lines of work for which the stress interview may be considered an appropriate weeding-out exercise. If you want to trade commodities on the Chicago Exchange, you deserve whatever they throw at you.

It has many names, but a "stress interview" is any interview in which the recruiter intentionally puts you on the spot simply in order to observe your reactions to an extremely high pressure environment. The questions asked are generally fairly standard, but they are phrased in unfriendly and menacing ways and are interspersed with assorted psychological tactics. For example, an interviewer might ask, "Give me *one good reason* why I should hire you despite your mediocre resume." and then dial the phone as you are responding. Short of hurling insults or physical abuse, there are very few limits to what stress interviewers will try.

I was once subjected to a stress interview, and I took the opportunity to give the recruiter a piece of my mind on the subject. That was not a good idea. While it may seem that the interviewer is trying to get a rise out of you, the exact opposite is true. What good would you be at work if your lost your head every time there was a crisis?

Stay calm. Assuming you want to make a good impression, keep your sense of humor—you shouldn't be cracking jokes, but a witty remark or two is fine. The best way to avoid punching the interviewer, while also not appearing a prideless sycophant, is to smile and let him think that you're enjoying it. And with the right attitude, it's really not so bad.

7. Energy and Stamina

The qualities of high energy and stamina, while required more extremely for some jobs than others, are sought by recruiters for every job. These characteristics are manifested in who you are and what you do, and you need to both *be* high energy and *act* high energy to impress most interviewers. Your résumé may have "active" written all over it, but if you slink through the interview with your eyes half open, you won't convince anyone. Likewise, even the most wired candidate still has to prove that all of that energy isn't expended worthlessly.

The second of these challenges is the easier one, and any half-decent interviewer should provide you ample opportunity to prove yourself a busy, productive person. Whether through the following questions or more general ones, you should be able to paint a picture of yourself as someone who moves from one activity to the next at breakneck speed, rarely needs eight hours sleep, and considers daily leisure time a thing of the past.

This impression should already be created by your résumé, which lists every extracurricular activity and campus job you ever touched with a ten-foot pole, highlighting your positions of leadership. Your verbal description of each activity must reinforce this feeling. Remember: Every task you took on was so challenging and time-consuming that it was only through extremely strict self-management that you were even able to go out with your friends on weekends.

But, as I've said, all your words mean nothing unless you've got the personality to back it up. It may mean avoiding morning appointments or drinking two cups of coffee, but don't go into an interview unless you're feeling "up." (No drugs, please.) Sit up straight during most of the interview and use your hands when you're making a major point. Speak enthusiastically in a low but strong voice and listen intently. Only then will you be convincing.

Like everything else, don't overdo it. If you have a tendency toward overenthusiasm (ranting and raving) keep it in check—an interviewer can be scared away if you try too hard. Your responses, while energetic, should not be long winded. If you're doing more than 80 percent of the talking, something's wrong.

Most questions in this category are fairly transparent, yet few candidates respond with truly impressive answers. The best responses make the candidate appear busy but organized, hardworking but content.

Q: **Describe your average weekday.**

A/E: Translated, this means, "describe your ideal weekday," which is not only full of activity, but well planned and with a sense of purpose. Mention your use of schedules, to-do lists, and any other time-budgeting tools. If you have a campus job, let it be known here, and also mention, if it's true, that you don't need much sleep.

Your average weekday should not involve going to a party. You can mention hating to miss a good film or concert (note the sense of determination), but you should otherwise steer away from discussing "unproductive" activities. An ideal statement would be: "I try to save most of my socializing for the weekends, but I allow myself a nice, long dinner so that I can relax with my friends before getting back to work." A candidate with *no* leisure time is intolerable.

Q: **How do you feel about sixty-hour workweeks?**

A/E: This question varies depending on the industry, but is an all-time favorite whenever the job has a set weekly salary. When I was looking for a job in investment banking, it was "eighty-hour workweeks," and I think that I may have developed the perfect answer (the sad thing is that I believed it at the time):

> "I look at it this way: Here I am at school spending forty hours a week on my studies alone. At the same time I've got three hours a day of sports, plus all of the responsibilities involved with my other activities. It's rare that I take a full weekend off, yet if I had anything less to do, I'd be bored.
>
> "When I leave here, I'm going to have to find something to replace all of the things that I do now—not just the classes, but the sports and other activities too. I can see how it would be different if I were older and had my own family, but, really, I should thank you for providing me with a way to keep busy."

Q: **Are you a workaholic?**

A/E: After the previous response, this question should come as no surprise. While you should certainly give a negative answer, keep in mind that most recruiters will hire whatever workaholics they can get their hands on. You may collapse at age forty, but that gives them fifteen-plus years of virtual slave labor. What could be more ideal?

A good response would stress the negative aspects of workaholism, and how those parts of the definition could not be applied in your case. You enjoy your friends and your limited leisure time, and you get a great deal of satisfaction out of your work.

Racism/Sexism

Despite all of the improvements that have taken place over the years, it's impossible to say that there is no prejudice in the job market. If you come across it, act according to your own conscience, but don't sink yourself in the process. Remember that your goal is to get the job offer. You can always turn a company down later— or make it pay a greater price (can you say "lawsuit"?)— but the interview is no time to make waves.

It has never happened to me, but were I faced today with an interviewer who made sexist or racist comments, I wouldn't smile and nod, but neither would I put the culprit on the spot. If the interviewer were particularly offensive, I would mention it to his superior, but *after* the process was over. Also, I would try to avoid condemning the entire firm just because it hired one bigot.

If, as a woman and/or minority group member, you are concerned about a firm's Equal Employment Opportunity record, I would again suggest waiting for an offer before asking any pointed questions. While you may be perfectly sincere in your concern, many interviewers will interpret your questions as an attempt to weasel your way in as a statistics-booster. The more antidiscriminatory a company is, the more it will see these questions as self-serving, if not paranoid.

On the other hand, if you yourself have a tendency toward cracking racist or sexist jokes, keep them to yourself. You may think, perhaps even correctly, that you are not prejudiced, but your interviewers can't read your mind. They will take everything they can the wrong way . . . as I had the opportunity to do on several occasions.

8. Maturity

It's true that there is a premium placed on youth in today's job market—you may find it difficult to land an entry-level position if you're over twenty-five. But, given that most applicants for the jobs you're seeking are themselves just past adolescence, the best candidates are often those who look and act the oldest. For people in their early twenties, both in getting the job and in getting promoted, a little grey hair is preferable to acne.

But since you can't do very much about acne, it is your actions that must make your maturity plain. Without sacrificing your enthusiasm or sense of humor, behave in a manner befitting a full-grown adult. The impression of physical maturity starts with such things as table manners and works its way down to how you sit, walk, and hold yourself. Can you picture your interviewer acting the way you do or saying the things you say? If not, you may be coming off as just another inexperienced college kid.

Of course, the maturity that recruiters are seeking runs much deeper than simply how old you seem to be. Do you plan ahead and make carefully thought-out decisions? Do you know what you want out of life? Are your goals realistic? Are they *adult* goals? Do you have a healthy conception of your own worth, as an employee and otherwise? These are the issues that recruiters address when attempting to determine your rating in this category.

Although an hour of self-analysis will accomplish little in making you a more mature person, it would be wise to spend some time pondering these questions. Keep them in mind when formulating your responses to the questions you can expect to receive in interviews. Simply knowing that you are being judged in this light puts you at an advantage.

Your maturity will be under a microscope during the entire interview, but especially when you hear any of the following:

Q: **What are your career plans?**

A/E: Also intended to gauge your interest in the job at hand, this question is primarily designed to determine the extent and realism of your plans. While expressing a carefree, "take it as it comes" philosophy will get you nowhere, you must realize that *compulsive* planning is an equally convincing sign of immaturity. If you have a tendency to make long-term plans that end up falling through, recognize that trait and avoid manifesting it here.

This question represents one of those instances in which the most mature thing you can do is acknowledge your youth. It takes a lot of insight to realize that as you get older your plans may change. To know at age twenty-one exactly what you will be doing in ten years is quite unusual. Still, you should at least have a tentative plan, and a good sense of how the job you want fits into it perfectly.

Q: **How did you choose your college?**

A/E: This question (and its cousin, "How did you choose your major?") is designed to expose your decision-making ability as well as the maturity of your goals. First, your response must make it plain that your final decision was logically and completely thought out. Reasoning such as "My mother went there" or "I had a fun visit" betrays a whimsical lack of determination.

Second, the factors that contributed to your decision must represent criteria that the interviewer respects. The best meal plan or a low state drinking age is no reason to pick a school—or if it is, it should never be admitted.

Of course, to be entirely objective in your response is to deny the human factor, and risk losing the interviewer as a friend. It's perfectly sensible to admit that a large part of your decision was simply determining where you were most comfortable; the same will be true for choosing between offers.

Q: What do you expect to contribute to this firm?

A/E: One fairly accurate measure of your maturity is your level of self-confidence. Although plenty of highly successful professionals have under- or over-inflated egos (more of the latter), finding your first job will be difficult without a realistic conception of what you have to offer, both professionally and in general. If you lack confidence, no interviewer will be impressed with you, and if you have too much confidence, no interviewer will like you.

Self-confidence is such a central factor in interviewing that it would merit a chapter on its own, were it not for the fact that there is very little that you can do about it. In the limited time that you have to find a job, you cannot hope to change your personality. The most you can do is force yourself into a position of healthy self-confidence by applying for the right jobs. Interviewing for positions that you know are highly competitive but that you also know *you deserve* should keep you from becoming excessively arrogant or meek.

Independent of the impression your attitude creates, interviewers still trust questions like this one to assess your self-confidence and maturity. Thus, you can counteract any of the recruiter's potentially negative impressions in this category by being prepared with some appropriately confident answers.

As with the similar questions discussed in section 5, you must still work toward modesty in your response. You'll get nowhere telling the interviewer that you'll contribute "phenomenal raw intelligence" to his firm, even if it's true. If you're intelligent, he already knows it. Talk about working hard, serving in whatever capacity they see fit, and taking on whatever responsibility you are able to earn. Also discuss specific education and work experience that will help you do a better job.

Q: **What is your worst quality?**

A/E: One indication of maturity is the ability to recognize your own imperfections and work to improve them. The trick with this question, if you haven't already guessed it, is to find and name a flaw that doesn't mar your desirability as an employee. Thus, a tendency toward laziness, irritability, procrastination, or pyromania is out of the question. Similarly unacceptable are any of those transparently propagandistic responses suggested by other job-hunting books. "I suppose I'm a bit of a perfectionist, and I guess I should learn to stop working myself so hard." Give me a break.

Unfortunately, this leaves you with very few acceptable answers. Your best move is to pick a minor vice with some positive ramifications and stress that you have been fairly successful in overcoming it. A good example would be:

> "Over the past few years I've come to realize that I can be a little bit impatient at times. I don't make people wait for me, so I really don't like to wait for anything myself. It used to really irritate me sometimes—I'd never lose my temper, of course, but it would cause me some stress. Anyway, I've learned that in most cases there's not very much that I can do about the object I'm waiting for— besides being persistent—so now I just try to keep my mind busy with something else."

Q: **What is the meaning of life? Why are we here?**

A/E: I doubt that you will hear this one, though it was one of my favorites. I mention it here so you'll know that anything is fair game in an interview. Prepare yourself for questions like this, and you won't be easily surprised.

A more common version: "What do you want out of life?" serves as another good test of maturity. Recruiters employ it to see if you've taken the time to develop a personal philosophy. They are probably quite sincere in wanting to know you as a complete person, whether they deserve to or not. Humor them.

Tell them your purpose in life, making sure that it's conducive to success at the job in question. I remember one candidate who responded with: "To love and be loved," his eyes glistening. While I admired his good intentions (and insight), I could hardly continue to consider him a future investment banker. I wanted a personal answer—but not a baring of the soul.

Emulation

Headhunters like to hire people who remind them of the men and women already working at their firm. The ideal candidate looks like he has already spent a year on the job. The trick, however, is to have the manner of a working person without any of the pretentions that can often come with it—the eighty-dollar ties or the slick trade jargon. A babe in the woods with good technical skills is more likely to be popular with interviewers than a big talker with clothes he couldn't have earned himself, even if the latter is a more familiar sight around the office.

So, try to emulate your interviewers, but remember that the towering height of my rejection pile was due partly to candidates who took that advice too far. I can remember at least two qualified candidates whom I tossed simply for referring to me, in the Wall Street jargon, as an "I-Banker."

9. Interest in the Position

Your interest—in the industry, the company, and the job—constitutes one of the areas of greatest concern to the recruiter. You can expect most interviewers to spend more time and ask more questions on this topic than on any other. Happily, it is a category in which you are largely able to determine your own fate.

In case you've heard otherwise: Your goal is, within reason, to appear as interested as possible. If the work doesn't thrill you, you can't very well be expected to do an excellent job—you might even turn down the offer (every recruiter's nightmare).

It is surprising, then, that so many candidates perform badly in this area. Either they lack interest and can't hide it, or they are unable (or unwilling) to let their interest shine through. In any case, you should have no trouble if you follow two simple steps:

1. State your interest candidly.
2. Prove your interest, by having done the necessary background research and by asking the appropriate questions.

There's really little else to it.

You will have ample opportunity to state your interest, mostly in response to a standard series of straightforward questions. By far the most common question in any interview is, "Why do you want a job in this field?" and you should definitely have an answer prepared. (As with all prepared answers, don't *over* prepare. A word-for-word memorization will never sound natural.) Regardless of the question, you need not be dishonest—just think about the job and be ready to discuss it in an articulate fashion. Don't hand out lines like, "I've wanted to be an assistant portfolio manager since I was ten years old." You will either be lying or boring.

For the details on background research, see chapter 3. Whatever amount of research you are able to accomplish—and you shouldn't have to do much—is futile unless used appropriately. Rattling off figures from a company's balance sheet will get you nowhere; an interested nerd is still a nerd. Rather, be equipped to carry your half of conversations pertaining to the job and the *relevant aspects* of the firm and industry.

Likewise, if the questions you ask refer to areas that bear little relation to the job or don't truly interest you, then you'll only succeed in puzzling the interviewer. Your questions, as discussed later in this chapter, must reflect a desire to learn, not to impress. Only then will your interest seem sincere.

The questions recruiters ask in this category take two forms: "Do you really want this job?" and, "Do you know enough about this job to really want it?" Because these questions are so popular, I have included a few extra ones here.

Q: **What fields are you investigating for employment?**

A/E: Unless the field for which you are interviewing is a tiny one, the proper response to this question is to simply name that field and no other. While it is not unusual for college seniors and recent graduates to simultaneously investigate, for example, investment banking, commercial banking, and consulting, most interviewers would consider this orientation too indecisive. Recruiters prefer people who know what they want, especially if what they want is to be like the recruiters.

With this in mind, you can see how one effective response

would be to describe a decision-making process that has resulted in your choosing the interviewer's field over another. For example:

> "I was considering employment in both the insurance industry and accounting—in fact, I was leaning toward insurance—until I spoke to a number of people in both fields, and our discussions made it very clear to me that the skills I would acquire in accounting would serve me much better down the road, no matter where my career may eventually lead."

In addition, certain industries look down upon other industries and won't consider you seriously if you mention them. Generally, consultants and investment bankers consider themselves superior to commercial bankers, who consider themselves superior to accountants and insurance people. When a candidate would mention to me that he was also interested in commercial banking, I would automatically assume that *a*) he didn't want to work investment banking hours, and *b*) he lacked confidence (perhaps with reason) in his ability to land an investment banking job. Thus, my opinion of him would fall considerably.

Likewise, though it may appear ambitious, telling an insurance interviewer that you are considering consulting is a risky proposition. Unsure of the desirability of his job over the consulting industry, he will fear losing you to a consulting firm, and thus no longer consider you a serious candidate. Also, connecting yourself to these firms—firms that he may resent—can put you in a bad light.

A more thoughtful response is that you *were* considering consulting, but you are no longer interested. This statement would suggest to the interviewer that you have the star quality that merits the more prestigious position, while also caressing his ego with the idea that you chose his industry over one considered more "elite."

Q: **What other firms are you interviewing with?**

A/E: Once you've told your interviewer that you have limited your job search to his field, this is liable to be the next question. Most candidates answer it incorrectly, by giving the interviewer a soap-operatic account of the trials and tribulations of their job search, complete with a list of the firms that have rejected them.

While this sort of information is extremely useful to the interviewer, it inevitably makes you look bad. Interviewers are usually looking to join the crowd, and they are more likely to accept another firm's opinion of you than their own. I can think of at least three times I rejected candidates with the thought in mind: "If Merrill Lynch doesn't want him, why should we?" Unless it's unavoidable, don't ever confide that another firm has turned you down.

Lying, as usual, is a bad idea, although stretching the truth a bit can't hurt. If an interviewer is so blunt as to ask you, "Have you been getting many interviews, callbacks?" and you haven't, it would be easiest to simply say no. But there's no harm in smiling and saying that things are going well, adding something like, "Of course, given all the luck involved, I can't say that I'm batting a thousand; but many firms seem to be showing an interest." The big mistake, the big lie, would be to either say, "No one's turned me down so far" (if it's not true), or to claim that you are being successful at specific firms where you have not done well. As I mentioned earlier, most interviewers have friends at other firms and may be aware of your progress there. However, to my knowledge, no recruiter has friends at *every* firm, so there's no real danger in implying that very few firms have turned you down.

If you already have offers at other companies, this is the time to mention them. Without seeming boastful, try to make each interviewer aware that you are in demand. But only mention these offers hand in hand with a reaffirmation of your sincere interest in the interviewer's company. A good way to phrase this sentence would be, "Well, I do have an offer outstanding from Liberty Mutual—and they hope to hear from me soon—but at this point I'm pretty convinced that I'd prefer to work here." And be prepared to explain why.

The only offers that you should *not* mention are those from firms that are considered vastly inferior or superior to the interviewer's. The same reasoning applies here as in the previous question. Naming inferior firms will make you look like a dud, and naming superior firms could intimidate the interviewer into rejecting you for fear of being rejected himself. It would also make you appear the idiot for preferring his firm over the other.

Generally, this question offers an excellent opportunity to present yourself as confident, modest, and realistic. My ideal answer goes something like this:

> "If I could have any job I wanted, I would only interview at a few firms, and yours would be one of them. But while I think that I'm a strong candidate, I realize how many other good people there are out there and how few jobs are available, so I'm not dumb enough to limit myself so severely."

Then you're free to mention any number of (decent) companies, within reason. This response sets you aside as confident in your candidacy, modest about yourself versus the other candidates, and realistic about the fickle nature of the process. And there is nothing like humble confidence to make the interviewer take a liking to you.

Q: **Strictly hypothetically, of course, if we were to give you an offer today, would you accept it?**

A/E: This is a nasty question and deserves a nasty response: "Yes." Or make them think yes, while leaving your options open. As stated earlier, even the largest companies hate giving offers that aren't accepted. Every turned-down offer forces them to lower their hiring standards just a little bit, and also puts their reputation in a bad light. But beyond that, no interviewer can deny the disappointment that comes from being told that the job—the product he's selling—isn't selling well. To tell an interviewer that you are "keeping your options open" is to suggest that not only is he peddling faulty wares, but also that he himself has perhaps made the wrong career choice. Or worse yet, if he works for a second-rate firm, that he must be a second-rate person.

This may all seem obvious, yet you'd be surprised how many candidates, while responding in a very cordial way, told me that they were keeping their options open. Somebody might have told them that this was the cool thing to do, to make themselves look confident and in-demand, but they were wrong. Nothing can send a chill through the room any faster.

The trick is to be as affirmative as possible without making yourself look hypocritical later when you don't immediately accept an offer. Don't give them an *unadulterated* yes unless you fully intend to take the job no matter what; broken promises have a way of sticking with you in the business world. The best response goes something like this:

> "Strictly hypothetically . . . I'd be thrilled. I've told you already that—from what I know so far—this would be my ideal place to work. I think I'd be tempted to take it right away . . . I might do that . . . but my conscience tells me that

I should at least keep the interview appointments I have next week, just so I know I'm making a truly educated decision. Yet, I can still tell you that there's a 90 percent chance that your offer would be accepted."

Feel free to be even more affirmative, to the extent that your interest in the company allows, but don't risk getting yourself in any binds for later.

Q: Describe your ideal job.

A/E: This one tests your imagination as well. Be as creative as possible without losing sight of the question's main purpose: to test your interest in the job at hand. Of course, humorous responses are not out of the question—"a product tester for Hershey's" is fine if you're not overweight.

But eventually you may have to respond seriously, in which case you should choose a future position that the currently discussed job will help you to achieve. Aim high, even beyond the bounds of what's reasonable, as long as you don't make them think that you *expect* the impossible. Remember: This is an *ideal* that we are talking about. And try to think of something besides "CEO of a Fortune 500 company." Starting your own firm is always attractive, especially if you have something unusual to sell.

Q: Can you tell me your current understanding of what we do here, in this division?

A/E: This was one of the most difficult questions I used to ask, judging by the number of candidates it stumped. You'd be astounded by how many candidates walk into interviews without the slightest understanding of the business they're attempting to enter. Have this question answered in your mind before you get to the interview. It's a nice touch to end your response with a request for further information.

Q: What do you see as the greatest problem concerning our industry right now?

A/E: Likewise, if you are truly interested in starting a career in a given field, you have probably developed some knowledge of its largest concerns. There is, of course, no single correct answer; your response should be presented as one of many possibilities. It's not so important what you choose to say, as long as you have some logical way to back it up.

Money

One of the biggest contradictions in the business world revolves around the attitude toward money. While everyone knows that you take a job in order to earn cash—and your bosses hope that your work will earn them loads of it—to admit a strong desire for money is considered hopelessly gauche. With rare exception, even the most cutthroat investment bankers, when asked about their lofty salaries, will grow quiet and mention something about having to put their kids through college. To earn money for the firm is admirable, but to want it for yourself smacks of the *nouveau riche* in an environment where cash is often more respected in the having than in the getting.

Only if you are interviewing for a job in which your salary will largely be determined on a sales-commission basis is it considered acceptable to rejoice in the innocent splendor of your greed. For insurance salesmen, stockbrokers, and bond-traders, a money-hungry attitude is seen as a key to success. But even in these instances, to dwell on the subject speaks of a lack of scruples. So, if you choose to bring up the subject, it is safest to mention it obliquely, such as: "Well, I want the job mainly because I know I'd enjoy it. But I also plan on working my tail off, so I'm attracted to the fact that your firm bases salary so strongly on performance."

For almost all jobs that don't pay on commission, how-ever, money is neither an adequate nor an attractive motivating factor. Any candidate who ever mentioned money to me in anything but an offhand way would not see our offices a second time. This includes such inno-cent, well-meaning statements as, "Frankly, I have a lot of college loans to pay off, and I realize that this will help me to do so." This sort of remark, though not necessarily an indication of greed, betrays improper motivation for the job.

Bearing the previous discussion in mind, it should be obvious by this point that discussing salary before you have the offer is strictly taboo. If information about salary is not circulating, and you need to know, try to find a source with no connections to your interviewers. Only if no source exists and no mention of compensation has been made—plus you fear the salary may be well below your requirements—should you consider asking about it. This situation, however, reflects a gross oversight on the part of the firm and is thus awkward for that reason as well. If you absolutely must ask, stick it in a "by the way" clause in your third or fourth question at the end of the interview, and have another question ready to change the subject afterward.

10. Personal Qualities and Personality

Listed on practically all recruiter review sheets, this category is a catchall designed to ensure the ultimate subjectivity of the interview process. *Personal qualities* refers to such peripheral factors as how you dress, how you behave at meals, and generally whether the interviewer considers you a trustworthy, well-adjusted, good person. *Personality* addresses whether or not you are someone whom the interviewer would want to spend time with and whether you would be likely to improve the atmosphere of the office. Together, these criteria ask a simple question: *Does the recruiter like you?*

With all the talk about qualifications and interest, many candidates do not realize that they are being judged in this category as well. Naively, they believe that the best candidate should get the job, independent of how the interviewer feels about them personally. As a result, they make no attempt to hit it off with the interviewer—they don't even begin to think of him as a person, much less as a possible friend. Don't make the same mistake. Without going so far as to sacrifice your professionalism, let your friendliness shine through (and if you're not naturally friendly, fake it). It may seem obvious, but: *Smile.* If you never smile during the interview, the recruiter is forced to conclude, disastrously, that you won't smile on the job. Be enthusiastic, energetic, and feel free to laugh now and then. Don't avoid telling enjoyable stories during the interview if they come naturally and are relevant. Make an attempt to like the interviewer; maybe he'll like you back.

As always, don't go overboard. Direct your sense of humor at something other than your interviewer, and get a feel for his mood before making any silly comments. Some people take themselves much too seriously. I once made a permanent enemy of a rather snobbish Goldman Sachs interviewer by joking with him despite his obvious lack of humor. Noticing that my twenty-five-dollar Timex was practically identical to his solid gold Patek-Phillipe watch, I commented, "Oh, I see we have the same watch." Being that the comment was at his expense (quite literally) and that the man was a serious stuffed shirt, he did his best to terminate my candidacy.

Of course, there are certain people who deserve to be taken seriously whether or not they do it themselves. The candidate who, when being introduced to the head of my division, cracked, "Nice suspenders, Mike," is probably still looking for a job. Never hide your friendliness and enthusiasm, but restrain your sense of humor when dealing with people who deserve a little extra respect.

Although your personality is rather obvious throughout the interview, there are nonetheless a tremendous number of questions designed to give interviewers a greater sense of whether they like you. As in the previous category, these questions are so common that I have included quite a few.

Q: **What do you do for fun?**

A/E: You'll also hear, "What do you do in your spare time?" and, "What are your hobbies?" As in the personal section of your résumé (if you need one), the more interesting your leisure-time activities are, the more appealing you are. Unlike in your résumé, it is now acceptable to mention such common activities as tennis or skiing, since your interviewer probably enjoys them as well.

So that you don't come off as a loner, mention at least one activity that is fairly social—even if it's just going out at night with your friends. Mental recreation, such as playing bridge or entering trivia contests, will give you an advantage in the *intelligence* column as long as it's nothing too nerdish. If your idea of a good time is attending MENSA meetings, then you could be in for some trouble.

Avoid mentioning hobbies like comic-book collecting and "Dungeons and Dragons," which at our age tend to indicate social retardation. And responses such as, "I like to spend the majority of my spare time doing extra reading about the insurance industry," suggest even graver personality flaws.

Q: Describe your ideal weekend.

A/E: This common question is not unlike the previous one, except for its use of the word *ideal.* It indicates a test of your imagination, so why not score some extra points by being prepared with a witty response? As long as you can make the answer sound spontaneous, you would be wise to ponder this question well before the interview.

Generally, active weekends are preferable to passive ones. Climbing a mountain is much more impressive than lying on the beach. Bring along a friend to earn those *team-player* points.

Q: How would your friends describe you?

A/E: Don't use this question as an opportunity to brag about your job qualifications, because your intelligence, creativity, and other desired qualities are not being tested as much as your relationships with other people. (Besides: Do your friends really care about your GPA?) There's no harm, however, in having your friends describe you as "busy, because we never get to spend as much time together as we'd like," as long as the response doesn't stop there.

Probably the best answer circles around *fun* and *trust:* You would expect that your friends consider you fun since you always seem to enjoy each other's company, and you *know* that your friends can trust you to help them out if they ever get into any trouble. The *trust* part of it may seem a bit dramatic, but evoking ancient chivalric codes seldom fails to impress even the most cynical recruiter.

Q: **How do you choose your friends?**

A/E: You might mention the concept of *trust* again here, but not with such stress that you end up seeming paranoid. One would hope that in this case it wouldn't be a concern.

The purpose of this question, if you haven't guessed it, is to weed out the snobs and the elitists. While few candidates are so inept as to bring up such qualities as physical appearance and family wealth, fewer yet realize that mentioning *any* such criterion can put them in a bad light. So . . . you like your friends to be intelligent, do you? Does that mean that you're unfriendly to those with less mental skill?

To succeed in business you must be able to make friends with anybody whatsoever, and your answer should reflect this ability. One ideal response would go like this:

> "Well, I can't say that I really *choose* my friends. I mean, who really knows why two people end up being friends . . . similar interests, philosophies? I think about my best friends, and I realize that none of them really has very much in common . . . different sports, different majors, different other friends. I guess they're just the people whose company I enjoy the most."

Q: **What's the funniest thing you've ever done?**

A/E: This question, and the next one, are favorites among interviewers who are getting bored with interviewing (that is: most of them). Its purpose, aside from discovering who is simply too insane to hold a job, is to determine whether a candidate will be at all entertaining around the office. Be prepared with an enjoyable story—nothing too racy.

Q: Tell me a joke.

A/E: Four out of five candidates whom I asked had no joke for me. It was very disappointing. Those who did, therefore, were at an immediate advantage, so have one or two ready.

Ultimately, this question is a test of not just your sense of humor, but your sense of propriety. Believe it or not, there are some quite funny jokes out there that are not racist, blasphemous, or overly racy. (A joke in bad taste is a joke on you.) How racy can you get? Here is an example of an interview-quality dirty joke that I picked up from a client's wife in Indiana:

Billy-Bob and Emma May were longtime residents of the community nursing home. One day Billy-Bob came rushing into Emma May's room, where she sat in bed reading.

"Emma May, do you know what day today is?"

"It's Friday."

"Why, sure it is, but it's also my birthday."

"Well, happy birthday to ya, Billy-Bob."

"Emma May, I'll bet you can't guess how old I am today."

"Well, Billy-Bob, I reckon I can."

"How you gonna do that."

"Well, my friend, I got myself a special method."

"OK, smarty pants, let's hear it."

"I'll tell ya, all right, but first you gotta take off your robe."

"Take off my robe?"

"Now, Billy-Bob, I can't guess your age unless you take off your robe."

"All right then." Billy-Bob took off his robe.

"Good. Now you gotta drop your drawers."

"My what?!"

"You heard me. Drop 'em."

"Well, you old loon, if you really think it'll help." He dropped his drawers.

"Now turn around three times." He turned around three times.

"Well, Billy-Bob, I reckon you're 82 years old today."

Billy-Bob jumped in surprise. "M-m-my gosh, Emma May, that's right! How in the Devil's name did you guess I was 82 years old?"

"Well," said Emma May, "it weren't too difficult, seeing as you told me yesterday."

One Nasty Trick

One mistake interviewees often make is to assume that big companies are like big, happy families, with each division working to the benefit of the others when it comes to things like hiring. In instances where different divisions *do* cooperate, you are likely to see one hiring system for the entire bunch, in which applicants are screened, selected, and perhaps even trained before being sent to their respective groups. Usually this isn't the case, however, and each division of a firm that does its own recruiting would like to grab all of the best candidates for itself. The result is an open competition, with a surprising lack of communication within the firm.

Often from this feeling of competition is bred a sense of disdain among interviewers toward their counterparts in other divisions. This is especially apt to occur when one group senses that another is more popular among candidates. Keeping this in mind, you would be wise to avoid taking interest in a firm's other divisions at the expense of the one you are interviewing in. If you are interviewing in division B because you fear that you may not get an offer from division A, keep this fact to yourself, if possible.

I used to take advantage of a neat little ploy to determine, somewhat jealously, the true intentions of the candidates I interviewed. I was recruiting for Public Finance at my firm, a division that some people investigated only because they were worried about not landing a job in Corporate Finance. Whenever I suspected from a candidate's résumé that he was truly interested only in Corporate Finance, I would say something like this:

"Well, as you know, I'm representing Public Finance, but I couldn't help noticing that your background points more strongly towards Corporate Finance. Now, my friends in Corporate Finance have told me to keep my eyes peeled for them, to see if I can find any candidates whom I think they'd like. If you'd rather that I send you on up to the folks in Corporate Finance than continue your candidacy within my division, I could perhaps work something out. Does that interest you?"

If the candidate responded with a "no"—as about half did—that he was truly interested in Public Finance, then I was quite pleased. If he said yes, then that was probably the end of him. Maybe I'd pass his résumé on to Corporate Finance, maybe I wouldn't. Very nice? No, but effective.

So, if you find yourself, as is often necessary, interviewing at firms *or divisions* that are not your top choice, keep your preferences under your hat.

Approaching the Interview

Having the right answers is essential to success in an interview, but it's only half the picture. You must also have an interview *strategy*. This strategy is not so much a specific battle plan as it is a sense of your role in the interview and your understanding of what an interview is meant to be. If your definition of the term *interview* coincides with the recruiter's definition, you are much more likely to be successful.

How Much to Talk   Any interviewer worth his salt knows that he should let you do most of the talking. Ideally, from his perspective, he would like to be speaking for less than 30 percent of the time, since his objective is to get to know you as completely as possible. (He doesn't care whether you know him.)

Although this strategy could not be called mutually beneficial, it is a mistake to try turning the tables, as some people suggest. If you know what you're doing (which you will, after this chapter), you should want the interviewer to get to know you a bit. If you speak for less than half of the interview, you will have trouble establishing yourself as a worthwhile person, let alone a significant candidate. And most interviewees' technique for limiting their participation is to use one-sentence answers, which turn interviewers off completely. When I was doing entry-level recruiting, the interviews in which I spoke the most were the ones where the candidates bored me so completely with short answers that I gave up on them early. All my talk was intended only to use up the remaining time before I could politely send them away forever.

But there is a difference between actively participating in an interview and dominating it. Never forget that it is the interviewer's job to set the pace and control the direction of the interview. Those who give up that job do so grudgingly. Given the entry-level nature of the positions you seek, you are not expected to express such strong initiative.

Part of avoiding control of the interview is to limit how often you answer questions with questions. This technique can prove quite effective in reducing your participation in an interview, but as a means of sidestepping tough questions it is *completely transparent*. Every now and then I would come across a candidate who refused to play the game by the rules, who thought he could outwit or impress me by answering none of my questions directly. Ultimately, it just made me mad. Only use this technique if you find yourself talking too much or if you need more information to provide an accurate answer—and don't use it very often.

A final point: When you're not so sure of what you're talking about, limit your words. Many candidates respond to the questions they can't handle by talking *more*. This approach is acceptable for trying to solve an analytical question out loud, but otherwise it can make you look very foolish. Why discredit yourself with a wordy, inane response? One sincere, "I honestly don't know'" can do wonders for your credibility.

The Positive Approach   While many interviewers may be offensive, you should not approach an interview with a defensive stance. I've had to sit through about ten interviews where the candidates shuffled into my office like wounded soldiers about to be interrogated by an enemy captor. They obviously equated interviews with torture—not a bad assessment, given their attitude. Needless to say, they didn't make it through the first five minutes, for a number of reasons. First, it's impossible to perform well with a negative attitude. Second, recruiters are looking for self-confident candidates who approach life enthusiastically. Most importantly, recruiters, like everyone else, want to have fun. If you depress them, they will not like you.

If you must, prepare yourself for interviews by running down your beautiful résumé and thinking about everything you have to offer. They granted you an interview, so they must like what they see. (If that doesn't work, think of how badly you need the money.) It's not my job to make you feel good about yourself, but believe me when I tell you that, within limits, it's necessary.

Enjoying the Interview I can't think of an interview in which I smiled and laughed and then *didn't* like the applicant. That doesn't mean that you should spend half an hour telling jokes, but don't overlook opportunities to interject a bit of tasteful humor (see section 10 in this chapter).

There is, of course, nothing wrong with a completely serious interview, but it is important to end the interview in a good mood—the recruiter's final impression of you may be all that he remembers.

Asking Questions

At the end of almost every interview, you will be given the opportunity to ask questions. Though this custom may have developed strictly out of courtesy for the candidates, it is now used by many interviewers as a means of judging applicants. You must therefore think of the question-and-answer period as one more chance to make a good impression. Since your questions are the last things that you discuss with the recruiter, they may be what he remembers the most about you.

That does not mean that you shouldn't use your questions to address the issues that concern you about the job. In truth, you probably have to be sincerely concerned about the answers if you want your questions to come off well. Before asking, however, you must consider each of your questions in light of how it is going to make the interviewer feel about you and your candidacy.

Mistakes It follows, then, that there are certain things you should avoid discussing. First of all, be careful that none of your questions betrays a weakness in any of the ten categories discussed in this chapter. For example, asking, "Are there many late nights in the office?" automatically gives you a zero in the *energy and stamina* category. Second, don't ask any questions that would suggest that your job is not your top priority. Stay away from the topics of salary, benefits, vacation, overtime, and anything else that smacks of "What's in it for me?" As mentioned earlier, the time to fully investigate those areas is after you have the offer.

Don't think of the question-and-answer period as an opportunity to turn the tables on the interviewer. It's true that you are in the driver's seat, but that only means that you have additional responsibility for any accidents. No matter how strong you think your candidacy is, you are in no position to ask the company to prove itself to you. If the interviewer feels that he or his firm is in any way being tested, he will immediately go on the defensive. Don't forget that the interviewer's impression of you is inextricably intertwined with the impression you give him of himself. To suggest doubt in his firm is to suggest doubt in him, and he won't like you for it. This is especially the case when it comes to such sensitive issues as lawsuits, falling stock prices, and critical press—don't bring them up.

Many candidates, for want of more questions, ask the exact same questions of every interviewer. This practice, which isn't necessary if you are well prepared, is rarely caught; recruiters are not in the habit of discussing candidates' questions. The mistake would be to repeatedly ask a question that is especially memorable, one that recruiters are likely to write down or share with each other. Of course, questions like "Describe your average day," which are designed to incite a variety of responses, can be asked over and over again without worry.

Finally, don't make the mistake of asking too many questions. Four is plenty, and eight is overkill, unless the interview has yet to reach the twenty-five-minute mark. Keep an eye on the clock, but even if the interviewer has run over, you should ask one or two quick questions when given the opportunity. If you make it plain that you know it's time to leave, your questions will seem all the more sincere. And saying, "I have more questions, but I don't want to make you late," is also a good way to suggest the possibility of a future meeting.

How to Ask Questions   The way you phrase your questions can be as important as the questions themselves. Don't ask for yes or no answers, or you risk having a stilted conversation. Give your interviewers the opportunity to hear themselves talk, by asking, "Can you tell me . . . ," or, "What do you think about . . . ."

Don't ask questions in a manner that indicates that you want to hear a specific answer. Exposing your desired reply before you hear the actual one could betray an incompatibility with the position—and get you a dishonest answer as well. For example, if you like the idea of getting involved in the international aspects of a business, it would be a mistake to ask, "Would I have the opportunity to deal with many foreign clients?" A "no" answer would be a bit embarrassing. Rather, ask "Would the majority of my work be on the domestic or the international side?" Whatever the answer, the recruiter need not feel like he's disappointing you.

In fact, you can take advantage of these neutrally phrased questions by responding enthusiastically to whatever answer you receive, even if it's the wrong one. "Domestic? Excellent. I'd really prefer to be able to concentrate on the U.S. market." A bit slimy? Yes—but worth considering.

Equally slimy and effective is the one exception to the neutrality rule: asking questions that you know have the answers you want to hear. If you are certain that the job requires a lot of travel, feel free to ask, "Will I be able to do much traveling?" In this case, there is no need to phrase it neutrally, since there is no risk of disappointment. When the interviewer responds in the affirmative, let your face reflect your satisfaction. "That's great. The more the better, as far as I'm concerned."

Topics for Discussion   Many questions are acceptable in almost any type of interview, but the best questions are those that are custom-made for the opportunity being discussed. These often develop naturally from the interview conversation. If you carefully consider what the interviewer is saying to you, rather than just nodding your head and smiling, your curiosity should provide these automatically.

But you needn't rely entirely on the interview to supply questions of this type. If you have done effective research on the industry and the position, you should be able to bring a few intelligent, germane questions with you. For example, if you have previously asked an information interviewer to name the biggest problem facing the industry, and he has told you "tax reform," then you can ask the recruiter something like, "Do you worry about tax reform as a real threat to the industry, or is that just a temporary concern?" Now *that's* a good question. As mentioned earlier, the main purpose of your information interview questions is to make you look good during the real thing.

While the industry is certainly worth discussing, most of your questions should deal with the job itself, since that's the main topic of the interview. There is nothing wrong with questions about the firm, but they should focus primarily on *the company as a place to work* rather than *the company as number such-and-such in its industry*. For example, "Why is BigBank's level of employee loyalty so high?" is much superior to, "Why is BigBank's level of foreign investment so high?"

Another good topic for questions consists of the interviewer himself. With few exceptions, these people love to talk about themselves. Indulge them with questions about their latest project, their biggest deal, and anything else business-related. Also, do them the honor of asking for their opinions. Remember that many of these people don't carry much weight around the office and are probably used to having their opinions ignored. Once again, indulge them. What are their favorite and least favorite aspects of the business? What do they like most about the job that you are applying for? Their own jobs? Where do they see the industry in five years? Don't be surprised if the interview runs a few minutes into overtime.

As a last topic, consider anything positive that you've heard about the firm, in the news or elsewhere. The more relevant it is to the job, the better, but it's hard to go wrong in this area. This topic could provide the *final question* that you are looking for to end your interviews on the right note. A good example would be: "I read in the *Journal* that your division has just picked up a lot of new management talent. Does that mean you plan to expand into some new markets?" Most interviewers will reply with an enthusiastic response that pleases them as much as it does you.

Some Sample Questions

As mentioned previously, the best questions are job-specific and cannot be applied indiscriminately. The following examples, however, should give you a good idea of what types of questions interviewers generally like to hear:

"How large are your typical client/project teams? Who are they composed of?"

"How long does a typical assignment last?"

"How many assignments would I be covering at any given time?"

"How are assignments handed out?"

"Can you define what my responsibilities might be on a typical project?"

"How does the company handle the training of new recruits?"

"What level of client contact should I expect on the job?"

"How much experience would I be expected to have before getting involved in client presentations?"

"What would be my role, if any, in the solicitation of new business?"

"Would I work mostly for one or two superiors, or a larger number of professionals?"

"Are there a number of different groups within the division that I might be assigned to?"

"What potential is there for eventual promotion?"

"In the long run, how much value is placed on a business school degree?"

5

Interview Concerns

Wrapping the Skills Package

I was more qualified for the job; why didn't *I* get it? If you find yourself asking this sort of question, then you are ignorant of what recruiters look for in a good hire. They see each candidate as a skills package, and one that must be well assembled and attractively wrapped. The wrapping, in addition to your appearance, consists of how you carry yourself and how you interact socially. Let's face it: If looks and social skills didn't matter, you'd be filling out questionnaires rather than going to interviews.

Also, a number of fate-influencing factors are simply beyond your control. If the recruiter gets hit with a migraine during your interview, there's not much you can do about it. There is one factor, however, that can be worked to your advantage: the time of day at which you schedule your interview.

This chapter addresses these peripheral but surprisingly significant points.

Appearance

The dispute still rages over whether interviews are truly won or lost in the first five minutes. Most interviewers with any experience will tell you this: Very few interviews are won in the first five minutes, but a large number are lost in the first five seconds, due strictly to the candidate's physical appearance. As a recruiter, I found that, as simple as it is to dress acceptably, there were always a few candidates who managed to screw it up.

Clothes can say a lot about the person wearing them, and rarely is any of it good. You want your clothes to keep their mouths shut. If they say anything at all, it shouldn't be "stylish" or "expensive," but "tasteful" and "good quality." This philosophy finds its way into the conservative "Women's Wardrobe" and "Men's Wardrobe" described later in this chapter.

Appearance doesn't stop with clothing; be sure to pay equal attention to accessories and grooming.

Accessories   Purses and small, simple pocketbooks are fine for women. Men: If you're not yet in the habit of carrying a wallet, it's time to start, and the place for it is in one of your suit jacket's inner chest pockets. You don't yet deserve to have a briefcase, but a leather portfolio (without handles) or notebook holder is a good idea for on-site interviews. On campus, you are not expected to carry much more than a notebook with a few extra résumés stuffed inside. Watches should be attractive but utilitarian and without huge faces.

Grooming and Makeup   Bring a comb and fix yourself up in a bathroom mirror before your interview. Wear your hair in a conservative style. I don't care if your swim team is going to Nationals—don't shave your head with the rest of them. Bone-heads, and even ROTC buzz-cuts, don't fare well with interviewers.

In mainstream corporate America, moustaches are rather rare, and beards are downright unpopular. At my firm, only the computer personnel grew beards, so pass up that option unless you want to be placed in a back room. Moustaches must be judged on a case-by-case basis. If you have a sturdy, well-grown moustache (men only), you needn't get rid of it; thin, shaggy ones, however, are red flags for geekiness. (Remember that dweeb in high school who used to help you with your science homework?) When in doubt, shave.

You've heard it before, women, but I'll remind you that someone *always* wears too much makeup. If you're not certain how much to put on, start conservatively and then see what your female interviewers are wearing. In your standard corporate office, the women with the most eye shadow, nail polish, and lip gloss are the novice secretaries. If that position interests you, apply your makeup accordingly.

The ideal job candidate has no smell. Men should wear no cologne or aftershave and only enough deodorant to cover up what needs to be covered. If unscented antiperspirant works for you, stop there. For women, perfume is not forbidden, but an overdose can lose you the job. Nothing used to annoy me more than involuntarily having my office fumigated.

Ultimately, just to be safe, you would be wise to ask your friends for their advice on your interview outfits, accessories, and grooming. Perhaps it does not speak well of the business world that appearances are so crucial, but you've got to display knowledge of the rules if you want to be asked to play the game. As a friend of mine who recruits for an insurance giant says, "A man in a sports jacket or a woman in a pantsuit is a noncandidate."

Men's Wardrobe

Suit Two-piece, single-breasted, navy blue or charcoal gray, wool or wool blend, solid or with thin pinstripes. Single-vent American-style cut is preferable to double-vent (British) or ventless (Continental).

Shirt All cotton, well-ironed, white or light blue, with a standard or button-down collar. The cuffs and collar should be the same color as the body, and stripes are only acceptable if they are light blue and disappear from a distance. Striped shirts should not be worn with striped suits.

Tie Silk in a simple stripe or repeating pattern, with no more than three colors. The background color should be neutral—navy blue and maroon are ideal. Bright yellow and pink ties are no longer popular; nor is the entire *power-tie* concept. The knot should be small, a half-Windsor or something simpler, but beware of tiny knots in ties of thin material.

Footwear Shoes should be leather, black, polished but not blinding, and in a simple or wing-tip style. Socks should be patternless and match your pants or shoes in color.

Women's Wardrobe

Suit Long-sleeved jacket, straight or pleated skirt, of grey or dark blue wool. Black is also acceptable if the suit, and its wearer, are not morose. Patterns are only acceptable if they are extremely subtle, such as a fine dress tweed. No dresses. The jacket should be tailored to fit. The skirt should be at or just below the knee. Without calling attention to itself, the suit should not be so plain as to make you look like a Russian Communist Party member. If possible, see what your female interviewers are wearing and go slightly more conservative.

Shirt White, or a pastel shade, in a material that does not look shiny or unnatural. Cotton or matte silk is ideal. Frills such as puffy sleeves and lace should be used sparingly, if at all.

Collar Should be fully buttoned. A collar pin, simple gold necklace, or small string of pearls is a nice touch. A colorful scarf is also acceptable if it is neither too bright nor displayed too prominently. Those thin collar-ribbons that only spinster librarians and job applicants tend to wear are fine unless combined with a completely bland outfit. Avoid larger bow ties unless you can tie them perfectly.

Footwear   Sheer stockings or pantyhose in a skin tone, or lighter (white stockings are acceptable if the suit is on the light side). The best shoes are simple pumps with a one-to-two-inch heel. (You can go higher if you don't feel tall enough, but make sure that you can still walk quickly and steadily.) Shoes should be of high-quality leather in black or the color of your suit.

Jewelry   Post earrings only. One ring at most per hand, and one bracelet if any. A tasteful lapel pin is fine, but not together with a collar pin.

Makeup, etc.   A face can use color, but not coating. No frosted or bright lipstick, eye shadow, or nail polish. Keep your hair out of your face, but take it easy on the hair spray and mousse.

Dressing DON'Ts

A list of the dressing mistakes I've encountered could easily fill an entire book. The short checklist below should give you a general sense of the type of clothing and accessories to avoid.

Item	*Reason*
Spike heels or elevator shoes	Tacky
Cleavage	Cheap
Punk haircuts	Irresponsible
Glasses with unusual frames	Flaky
Sun-sensor or other dark glasses	Secretive
Brown suits (except tweed for women)	Gauche
Polyester	Gauche
Wide lapels and ties	Gauche
Expensive pens; pens in front shirt pockets	Showy; nerdy
Phi Beta Kappa keys or other advertisements	Insecure
Large costume jewelry	Kitschy
Diamond studs or other very expensive jewelry	Loaded
Monograms or cuff links	Loaded
Hermes ties or five-hundred-dollar suits	Loaded
Suspenders or exposed pocket handkerchiefs	Elderly
Unkempt or extra-long nails	Out of it
Men's collar bars or lasso ties	Out of it

Interview Etiquette

Most interviewee etiquette errors result from nervousness or simple negligence. You'll find that one year on the job matures your manners to a greater extent than four years in college. You begin to hold doors open for others, talk without cursing, and pick up the tab, not to mention referring to "girls" as "women" (which will leave your nonworking classmates dumbfounded). The trick, for now, is to fake it convincingly until it comes naturally.

Many questions of etiquette concern general behavior rather than simply manners, and are mostly common sense. I mention them here only because they are often confused or forgotten.

Timing Keep good records of all your interview times, especially the callbacks. Interviewers are not impressed by candidates who call them to "recheck" a forgotten interview date. Don't arrive late to your interview, of course, but also don't arrive more than fifteen minutes early; you don't want to look like you have nothing better to do with your time. For on-site interviews, get to the building half an hour early, make sure you know your way around, and then go get a cup of coffee (but not coffee-breath or jitters). Show up at the receptionist's desk five minutes before your interview.

If you know that you are going to be late, the time to act is beforehand. Call the office with an apology, a beyond-your-control excuse, and an estimated time of arrival. Messing up your interviewer's schedule will not ruin your chances, but keeping him waiting in the dark will.

Secretaries Treat the interviewer's secretary with more respect than if he were your own. Even once you've gotten the job, maintaining the secretaries' favor is key to your success with the firm. I, for one, would often ask my secretary what he thought of a candidate that I had just interviewed. Besides, whether I asked or not, he'd usually tell me.

Seating Most interviewers will ask you to sit down, but if one doesn't you should sit when he does (and never before). Whether he knows it or not, your standing above the interviewer will make him nervous. When given a choice of seats, choose the one closest to the interviewer, unless it will put you right on top of him. Avoid chairs that are much higher or lower than the interviewer's. Don't ask or dillydally about which chair is appropriate—it's awkward and suggests that you see the interview as a test rather than a meeting.

Privacy You should be friendly with the interviewer but not chummy, and his personal life is none of your business. Unless he brings it up, pictures of his family and other such items are not topics for conversation. Certain parts of the office are also off limits, like the area behind the interviewer's desk. Also, do not lean or place your notebook on the desk—it's not yours. Even if you're kept waiting, stay where you belong. Likewise, the only documentation that could possibly concern you is the magazines left for visitors and the pictures that the company has hung on the walls.

During the Interview Maintaining the necessary amount of eye contact should be easy if you really think about what the interviewer is saying rather than the fact that you are looking at each other. When you are speaking, a thoughtful look away now and then can be effective, but not if it doesn't come naturally;

you should usually speak to your interviewer's eyes. Also, keep your hands (and feet) away from your mouth when you talk.

Don't fidget, if you can help it. When I was job hunting, I once spent an entire interview playing with an ashtray, something I didn't realize until the very end. By that point it was too late.

Finally, taking notes during the interview will make you look like a nerd. Write down only what you need to know and won't be able to remember.

Names   Two factors have recently thrown the axiom of *Always use last names* into doubt. First, interviewers are becoming younger and younger, particularly if they currently hold the job that you are seeking. It seems silly to call someone "Mr." or "Ms." if they are twenty-two years old and one year your senior. Second, many companies are beginning to pride themselves on a "collegial corporate culture" in which first names are always used. My bosses were called "JoAnne" and "Betsy," and the head of my division was simply "Mike," despite the fact that he earned twenty times my salary. It seems a bit strange to refer to your interviewer by a name that he never hears on the job.

Being called "Mr." or "Ms." when one doesn't expect it is a bit of an honor, but it also puts the interviewer in a superior position. When a candidate would call me "Mr. Speck," I would think of him as polite and kind but also young and innocent, and by no means my equal. It was one of those rare instances when a candidate could make me feel good about myself without making himself look better in the process.

First names, therefore, are probably appropriate for interviewers who appear to be twenty-five or below, especially if their titles are fairly equivalent to the one you seek. For older and more senior interviewers, use "Mr." or "Ms." without fear. Most will tell you to use their first names anyway, but you have to watch out for those who would prefer the extra respect.

Using Names   Using an interviewer's name in conversation is effective if done once but becomes transparent if done repeatedly. The proper time to show an interviewer that you remembered his name is in greeting and leaving. Otherwise, he'll know what you're up to.

Remembering names, unfortunately, is quite important. Interviewers, passing you in the hall, will greet you by name. If you've forgotten theirs, it's almost impossible to hide it. There are many tricks for remembering names; I've noticed that if I can recall the name five minutes into the interview, I can usually remember it all day. The tough part is getting the name to register during the introduction, while you're worried about your handshake. This takes an extra conscious effort, but it's worth it.

Habits, Etc.   Don't smoke, don't ask to smoke, and don't even let anyone know that you smoke, even if they smoke themselves. Smoking stinks up offices and raises the cost of company medical insurance. It also indicates a lack of common sense and/or willpower, not to mention a possible tendency toward addiction.

I've found that gum-chewing before an interview, if you enjoy it, can help to get your confidence up—just remember to get rid of the gum before your name is called. Generally, keep your mouth incredibly clean and then *don't worry about bad breath.* The worry can be more damaging than the breath itself. If you sometimes get cotton-mouth, then bringing along a roll of mints is a good idea. It's bad manners to suck on a Lifesavers during the interview, but that's preferable to not being able to speak. Offer one to the interviewer and apologize for a dry throat.

Finally, you should leave an interview with a smile, a handshake, and a knowledge of the company's notification schedule. If the interviewer has neglected to tell you, then you have every right to ask when you might expect to hear from him. Don't imply that you *expect* to see him again, but to leave the room without some thought of the future is to admit defeat.

Thank-you Notes   Sadly enough, in today's job-hunting scene, thank-you notes are unnecessary. Half of the candidates my firm hired last year didn't send a single thank-you note, and the rest need not have done so. Moreover, the simple fact is that almost all interview decisions are made the day of the interview, if not during the interview itself. Any interview process that allows more than three days to elapse between interview and decision is half-baked, and any interviewer who waits that long won't be interviewing for much longer. By the time your letter gets to the post office, your fate has been determined.

This doesn't mean that you shouldn't send thank-you notes, but rather that you should be aware that their effect is once-removed: If you do happen to be invited back to the firm for another round, *this* is when your first thank-you note can help you out. A captivating thank-you note can win you an ally for the rest of the hiring process. Unlike all other correspondence, it is a means of *personal* communication; where possible you should use it to make friends.

A thank-you note that doesn't make you more likeable is about as useful as a blank résumé. Unless you make some egregious spelling error, it will be filed away and forgotten. An example of this sort of typical, useless thank-you note follows. If you plan to write notes like this one, don't waste your stamp money sending them.

Useless Thank-You Note

Dear Ms. Fire,

Thank you very much for our interview last week. It was both enjoyable and informative and gave me a good sense of the accounting industry and Numbers-R-Us. I remain convinced that your firm would be a great place to start my career after graduation.

If I can provide you with any additional information, please feel free to write or call me. Thanks again, and I hope to speak to you soon.

Sincerely,

Ivan T. Job

Successful Thank-You Note

Dear Jeff,

I just wanted to drop you a note to thank you for all the time and effort you put into making yesterday such an enjoyable day for me, and for the other candidates as well. Your relaxed attitude enabled me to be myself and feel very comfortable throughout the interview. It had never really occurred to me that interviews could be enjoyed.

It is going to be difficult for any other company to rival the impression I have of BigBank, both in terms of the job itself and the people in the company. I especially appreciated your honest comments about working in New York, and BigBank in particular.

Again, thank you for everything, and please extend my thanks to Mike and Brian as well. I look forward to hearing from you soon.

Sincerely,

Kay Sass

The likeable thank-you note, the one that wins you support at the firm, succeeds because it remembers what a thank-you note is: a sincere expression of gratitude. In the dozens of thank-you notes I received, I can remember only a few that actually made me feel *thanked.* As with interviews, your goal is to make the decision-maker feel good about himself, associate you with this feeling, and like you because of it.

There are many ways to accomplish this, the most direct of which is to make him feel like he's done you a favor. However, the nature of this favor is very important. If you imply that he was doing you a favor by granting you an interview, then you are saying that you didn't deserve one. Rather, you should make him believe that he, through his own skill, sensitivity, generosity, etc., was so helpful during the interview that you feel compelled to thank him. The sample *Successful Thank-you Note* contains the text of a letter I received last year. Following these principles, it made me want to hire the candidate on the spot.

Was Kay (not her real name) shoveling it on, or what? Did she lay this sort of story on everyone she interviewed with? I don't think so (I hope not), but it doesn't matter whether she was sincere or not. I bought it. Not only did I save the letter for posterity, but I sent copies to Mike and Brian (using the excuse that they had been mentioned) in order to give myself some good publicity. Her letter made me feel good, and it made me look good, which made me feel even better. By the time she came to New York for the final round of interviews, Kay's name was well known, since I had told many of my friends at work how much I liked her.

Of course, when you use this approach you are treading a fine line. You have to ask yourself how enthusiastically grateful and complimentary you can be without coming off as insincere. (As they say, if you can fake sincerity, you've got it made.) As a general rule, it is not a smart idea to write something that you don't at least partially believe. My interview with Kay had indeed been an enjoyable experience. If we had had trouble communicating, if Kay had been excessively nervous, or if the interview had been unpleasant, her letter would have been a flop. I would have thought her a complete sycophant and probably thrown her out of the process. But in her case, the compliments worked, because I believed that she meant them. If an interview is not at all enjoyable, don't bother sending this kind of thank-you note, or any at all. It would be a waste of time; you're probably already out of the process.

Sometimes, an interview that is not enjoyable may still be successful, as in the case of a "stress interview." These are not meant to be enjoyed, but you can usually get a sense of whether one went well or not. If you think that you may have been successful, the *Successful Thank-you Note* still applies, if it's fine-tuned to the situation. Rather than thanking the interviewer for putting you at ease, give him credit for presenting you with an exciting challenge.

Once again, don't lie. If you have nothing nice to say, don't send the letter. If you do, be sure not to go overboard. Remember: You don't want to seem insincere, and you don't want to betray your feelings of inferiority by being overly complimentary.

The Handshake

As effectively as wearing overalls to your interview, a limp or clammy handshake can terminate your candidacy before you even get a chance to sit down. Not only is it just plain unpleasant, but it also says a lot of things about your personality that you'd rather not have revealed. Even if your first interview does render you nervous, weak-willed, and insecure, there's no reason to betray that fact before you begin speaking.

Likewise, the bear-grip or moray-eel handshake, while less disgusting, can be equally offensive. I have actually had my hand injured by overenthusiastic candidates, and my pleasure at their sincerity was quickly quelled by the throbbing pain at the end of my wrist.

For both women and men, the perfect handshake is firm yet relaxed, strong yet restrained. It lasts approximately one second and peaks in grip strength just before the release. A quick up-and-down motion coincides with the grip and release. The hand is dry, not sweaty—as mentioned earlier, keep a handkerchief or tissue hidden in your pocket if this tends to be a problem.

Women deserve the same handshake as men. Male candidates must realize that many woman executives do not take kindly to any treatment that distinguishes them from their male counterparts. (Holding doors for women is fine, since you should do the same for men.) Dainty finger-grip handshakes are really no more acceptable than a kiss on the wrist, given the circumstances.

If you are uncertain of your handshaking technique, and even if you're not, practice with one or two of your friends. The statistics say that a number of you reading this book have unacceptable handshakes and don't know it. If you remain in doubt, just shake your interviewers' hands the way that they shake yours.

Time of Day

If your schedule is flexible enough, you should try to catch your interviewer during one of the best parts of his day. While every person has an individual rhythm, a full day of interviewing is strenuous enough to draw certain similar responses from almost everyone who tries it. A few recruiters might recognize this fact and consciously work to counteract their natural tendencies. For most, however, a typical day of interviewing would probably run as follows:

9:00 A.M. Warmup. Whether or not he's a "morning person," the interviewer needs some time to get going and can hardly be expected to be on his toes for the first interview. More importantly, he is not likely to be in a very good mood, especially in the case of on-campus interviews. If this visit consists of anything more than a day trip, then he and his buddies were out drinking last night on the company tab.

9:45 A.M. By the middle of his second interview, the recruiter has worked out most of his aggressions, gotten into the swing of interviewing, and become seriously interested in finding three to five candidates that he can invite to the callbacks. He is at the top of his game and is beginning to enjoy himself.

11:00 A.M. After his fourth interview, the recruiter's breakfast, if he had one, begins to wear off. He realizes that lunch is still pretty far away, he's already beginning to get tired, and he's got almost a full day of interviews left ahead of him.

11:30 A.M. Optimism boost. The recruiter is still tired, but the last interview before lunch can only be seen as a positive experience.

1:30 P.M. The afternoon's cycle mirrors the morning's, with the slow start resulting this time from having to digest lunch. This could be the day's lowest-energy interview.

2:30 P.M. The interviewer realizes that his day is two-thirds over, and lunch is no longer troubling. Attention turns again to the callback quota, which has yet to be filled.

3:30 P.M. Burnout. By this point one face begins to blend into the next, and the recruiter is certain that he's interviewed several candidates at least twice. Only the most interesting candidates will catch his attention at this hour.

4:30 P.M. The last interview of the day is a time for jubilation and also the time for last-minute quota-filling. But what if he's already got enough favorites? It's worth the risk because he probably hasn't. Besides, he can always change his mind or add one more if he really likes you. And at five o'clock there's a good chance that he'll like you a lot.

In a nutshell, aim for the early mid-morning, the early mid-afternoon, and the spots immediately preceding lunch and happy hour. Chances are that you'll be at *your* best during the same times, but if you know otherwise, take that into account. Also, your instincts regarding days of the week are correct: If you have a choice, interview on Thursday or Friday. (Avoid Friday *afternoon*, however, as people are often rushing to complete their week's work.) Finally, remember to sign up for your interview early, before all the best spots disappear.

Femininity

Sometime soon, probably before the year 2000, the words *femininity* and *professionalism* will lose what little remains of their contradictory meaning. For women entering the job market today, however, the femininity issue remains a difficult one.

Although it may seem hard to believe now, it was only as far back as our parents' generation that significant numbers of women began to join the "men's club" that was corporate America. Through no fault of their own, most of the women who did so had to become "one of the boys," shedding many of the characteristics that distinguished them from their male counterparts. They made it into the boardroom, but their femininity did not.

Within the last decade the situation has changed considerably. Women have established positions of significant power that allow them to act any way they damn well please, just as men do. While it is, of course, still acceptable to behave in a more "masculine" way, the men and women that now constitute the *establishment* have begun to accept the idea of a thoroughly feminine executive. But that revolution is not yet complete.

What this means for the job-hunting alumna is fairly simple: If the rules of the road—as outlined in this book and elsewhere—seem a bit stifling to your femininity, that's the main concession that you will have to make to the incomplete status of women's liberation. It's not so much sexism as the legacy of sexism, and it's probably quite temporary. In the meantime, you would be wise to dress and act conservatively until you've got the job. If you want to change the system, you have to infiltrate it first.

6

The Callback Interview

More Than "More of the Same"

The callback interview is the final step between you and the job. If you've made it this far, you have almost a 50 percent chance of receiving an offer; all you have to do is impress the remaining interviewers as much as you did the first. Usually, that means not changing your act significantly. Whatever you did the first time worked, so you would be wise to stick with it.

There are a few factors, however, that distinguish callbacks from first-round interviews. The interviewer's *purpose* is usually not quite the same, and you must deal with a variety of *players*, each of whom wants something slightly different from you. You should be aware of these distinctions so that you are prepared to respond appropriately.

Purpose

There are essentially two types of formats for callback interview schedules: *structured* and *unstructured*. The latter is much more common, but you should be prepared for both.

Structured Callbacks In a structured callback schedule, each interviewer is asked to investigate a different aspect of your candidacy. One may be assigned *intelligence and skills*, another *experience and interest*, a third *personal qualities*, and so on. You may even come up against a staff psychologist.

The purpose of these interviews is often the exact opposite of your first-round interviews. No longer is the recruiter looking specifically for a well-rounded candidate, someone who will satisfy many different interviewers' investigations of many different qualities. Rather, he is looking to satisfy only himself on only a few qualities. He may notice a glaring problem that is outside of his jurisdiction—and if he does, he will make a note of it—but he won't actively attempt to rate you on anything but his assigned area.

Since this recruiter does not have a ten-point evaluation sheet in front of him, your strategy is changed considerably. No longer should you make a point of exhibiting the full spectrum of your qualifications. In this case, changing the subject to a "neglected" category will simply frustrate the interviewer's attempts to do his job. Allow yourself to be carried by the flow of the interview, and take the time to discuss his questions on a more profound level.

Unstructured Callbacks   An unstructured callback schedule is in many ways like a series of first-round interviews. Aside from handing out evaluation sheets to the different interviewers, the recruiting coordinator goes to little effort to organize the information collected. Most callbacks, including the ones at my firm, are of this type.

Your goal here, since each interviewer is asked to come up with an overall evaluation, is to reproduce the well-rounded picture that you painted in your original interview. Don't be surprised, though, if some of the lines of questioning you face are rather unorthodox (*e.g.:* "If you were an animal, which would you be?"). Conservative approaches are usually left to the first-round interviewers.

Here, as in the structured interview, each interviewer is interested only in satisfying *himself* with your qualifications, and thus he is not as likely to get the whole picture. He still has to fill out the review sheet, however, so any help you provide will probably be appreciated. Once again, though, refrain from taking control of the interview.

The trick, obviously, is knowing whether your callback is the *structured* or *unstructured* type. The best way to find out is to ask. When you telephone your first-round interviewer for information (see "Callback Preparation," later in this chapter), manipulate the conversation to the subject of interviews and interviewing techniques. If the discussion runs smoothly, it shouldn't be awkward to ask something like,

> "I'm curious . . . . For your callbacks, do you folks just conduct a number of first-round-style interviews, or do you assign different tasks to different interviewers?"

The recruiter has no reason not to answer you, especially since your success can only make him look better. If you are not able to comfortably ask this question of your interviewer, try to find the answer through the graduate grapevine. It is definitely worth knowing. Happily, many interviewers will inform you of their company's callback structure before you even get a chance to ask.

Surviving a Full Day of Interviews

There are two main obstacles to continuous high performance in callback interviews: fatigue and boredom. They usually surface around mid-afternoon, which is early enough to sink your overall score. If your four-o'clock interview is with an *energy and stamina* fanatic, you may as well hide in the bathroom.

Fatigue Answering interview questions for six or more hours is one of the toughest things you will ever do. While there may be temptations to behave otherwise, be sure to get a good night's sleep beforehand. I have seen several qualified candidates fall on their faces due to hangovers and general grogginess. If your corporate hosts want to take you out the night before, you have no choice but to go along. But take it easy on the drinks and politely get yourself to bed by midnight.

Your morning dose of coffee depends on your current level of addiction, but avoid drinking extra cups to get yourself started. Too much coffee in the morning practically guarantees an afternoon crash. Be especially careful if coffee is kept brewing all morning long; they get you hooked, and then at lunchtime they take the pots away. (A nasty trick.)

I'll gladly be the tenth person to tell you: Eat a good, medium-sized breakfast. Not only will it improve your morning performance; it will save you from the embarrassing "11:30 stomach-rumbles." It can also prevent you from devouring a huge lunch, that being the biggest mistake in interviewee nutrition. The company may provide a wonderful spread, but lunch is not the time for carbo-loading, unless your interview schedule includes an afternoon nap time. Eat the same amount that you usually do, or a little bit less.

Boredom After a few interviews, you realize that most interviewers ask the same questions. The interviewers are aware of this fact as well, but they choose not to do anything about it. Unless you are lucky enough to receive a *structured callback*, every interviewer is going to ask you why you want the job.

This situation is advantageous in that it fosters the development of thoughtful, well-phrased answers. Unfortunately, it also eventually bores you to death. As your responses become more rehearsed and you become less interested, you begin to sound like a history professor on Quaaludes. Combine this with the fact that the interviewer has probably heard the same answers before, and you've got all the ingredients of a stalled interview.

There's not much that you can do about your boredom but make an effort to hide it. Remember, you've never had the chance to talk to this person before (and you might never again). If you can't feel enthusiastic, fake it. An animated tone of voice is often all it takes to conceal a dull state of mind.

The Players

The callback interview puts you face to face with one of the toughest aspects of business: presenting yourself in an appealing manner to a variety of people, each of whom expects something different from you. A few weeks on the job will teach you much of the ideal way to behave. But for now, judging by the number of candidate faux pas I've witnessed, a few tips are in order.

The Entry-Level Employee   This is the person with whom you are going to be working and socializing, and you could say that above all he is considering you as a possible friend. Because of this, he is probably most concerned with learning whether you are fun, interesting, and amiable. In interviews, however, he is almost always your toughest customer. You are being considered for the position that he currently holds, so he must think of you as his equal if he is going to give you the stamp of approval. After all, if a flawed candidate can make it through the process, then he himself could be flawed, which is unthinkable.

Your job is to always be friendly with this person—especially when you're not in an interview situation—but not to let that get in the way when it comes time to prove your qualifications. Also, the entry-level employee is rather proud of his job, so it wouldn't hurt to subtly glorify the position you are applying for. If it is at all true, mention the job's high level of responsibility and tell him how you envy his opportunity to make significant decisions.

The Middle-Management Employee This is the person whom you're going to be working *for*, and he, above all, is looking for happy slaves. Unlike your entry-level interviewers, he is likely to be turned off by talk about high responsibility and decision-making. After all, if *you're* making the decisions, who's crunching the numbers?

As far as middle management is concerned, you should understand that the job of an entry-level employee is simply to do whatever his superior asks of him. You realize that there are going to be a lot of unglamorous assignments. That's fine, because you see an entry-level job as a chance to *pay your dues* while gaining the experience necessary to get ahead.

Stress your willingness to roll up your sleeves and to stay late. You should still create an impression of friendliness and competence, but spend extra time extolling the virtues of hard work.

The Senior Employee Due to his relative power, the senior employee often feels less obligation to follow the rules, so he is less likely to use any prescribed guidelines for rating you. Rather, he'll just decide whether he *likes* you or not. While all ten of our rating categories may come into play, this interviewer is going to pay more attention to your personal qualities. He thinks of employment as a long-term proposition, and will try to decide if you fit his concept of a *company (wo)man*. Not only must you possess the necessary skills, you must also demonstrate the integrity and thoughtfulness that people who have *made it* realize are important.

If you are lucky enough to be interviewed by a senior employee, recognize the honor and behave appropriately. Don't let obsequiousness get in the way of your interview performance, but pay respect where it's due.

The Personnel Employee Most firms insist that you speak to at least one member of the personnel department before receiving an offer. This person's function can vary widely. He could be a staff psychologist, but then again, he could just be one more addition to the general interviewing team. At my firm, the personnel department member was included simply for his greater interviewing experience, but at most corporations this is not the case. Usually, the personnel person functions as a screen, someone to get around. As such, he can do you little good.

Unless you get the impression that he is serving as "just another interviewer," the personnel person should be approached with a defensive strategy. Don't take any wild chances in hopes of impressing him. If he loves you, it doesn't matter; all you care is that he doesn't dislike you. There's no need to change your personality, but a little extra conservatism couldn't hurt.

The First-Round Interviewer   There is no doubt that the person who invited you back for the second round is your ally, but don't try to take advantage of that fact. He would love to see you succeed, but the last thing he wants is for his colleagues—or any other candidates—to think that he is playing favorites. I remember feeling particularly resentful toward one candidate who spent much of the callback trying to show what great buddies we were, acting as if the two of us shared some sort of special secret. That embarrassed me, and it had an even worse effect on him.

Your first-round interviewer deserves a warm greeting, a status report at the end of the day, and a "thank you" for whatever additional help he provides. Otherwise, don't trouble him any more than he asks to be troubled.

The Alumni Acquaintance   Similarly, don't think that four years of rooting for the same football team makes someone a friend for life. If a current employee *was* your friend at college, then treat him appropriately. Aside from that, however, a shared alma mater merits little more than a casual conversation. Take whatever special treatment he offers, but don't expect anything.

In interviews, don't drop the name of an employee acquaintance unless you're sure that he has good things to say about you. Anybody you mention will probably be consulted before decision time.

Other Candidates   If there are competing candidates interviewing at the same time as you, treat them as you would your future colleagues. You cannot afford to think of them as adversaries. The friendlier you are to everybody, the better you look.

Callback Preparation

Callback preparation is even easier than first-round preparation because this time you already have someone who is able and willing to help you: your first-round interviewer. Since he wants to see you do well on your callback, he is not likely to turn down a polite request for assistance.

Call him in the late afternoon, when he is least likely to be busy, during the week immediately following your callback notification. (Chances are you have to call him anyway to arrange your office visit.) Ask him if he has any additional information that he can send you about the job, the company, the department he works for, or anything interesting that you discussed during the interview. You should plan to read whatever he sends—if he sends nothing, don't worry—but realize that the real purpose of your phone call is to get a conversation started.

No doubt the interview has raised some new questions in your mind about the job. Ask them and see where they lead you. If your interviewer holds the position you are applying for, ask him about the work he does. If he's a more senior employee, *ask him for the name of an entry-level hire with whom you can talk.* Then, give this person a call, and ask *him* about his work. As long as you are polite and enthusiastic, you'll end up with more information than you know what to do with and a new contact as well.

More Interview Questions

Most of the questions that you hear in first-round interviews are fair game in callbacks, and vice versa. With all questions, the same general rule applies: Before answering, think about what the interviewer is trying to evaluate and what your answer will really tell him.

You can add the following questions to your repertoire:

- **Why should we hire you?** Mention hard work, experience, and record of achievement, but don't brag.

- **Why will you do well on this job?** Same idea.

- **Why will you enjoy this job?** Your research will come in handy here. Mention the challenge, but also cite something job-specific.

- **I'm going to review you in six months. What criticism will I have?** Mention previous reviews in which you were spotless. Otherwise, treat this one like "What is your worst quality?"

- **Name a major problem you have solved at work.** Have one ready.

- **You are about to head off on your ideal weekend, and an office emergency forces you to cancel it. How do you feel?** You should be disappointed, but you've got your priorities straight and work comes first.

- **Did you work during the school year to provide some of your college tuition?** If you did, it should probably say so on your résumé. If you didn't, mention summer jobs and the activities that kept you so busy during the year.

- **Do you plan on getting an MBA?** Before you get asked this question, find out what they want to hear.

- **In what environment do you like to study?** You do your best work with other people around (unless they plan on giving you your own office).

- **Tell me about yourself.** Direct your response toward your work-related qualities.

- **Tell me about your family.** Keep it short. Don't lie, but don't reveal any dark spots. Your family is hard-working, principled, and supportive.

- **Tell me about your childhood.** Another stupid question. Don't treat the interviewer like a psychologist (unless he is one). Once again, don't let your guard down too far. A difficult childhood can be a plus, but not if it is the sort that would leave you traumatized.

- **Who in your life has had the greatest influence on you?** Pick an appropriate role model, someone close to you who believes in the value of a good day's work. Stress ethics as well.

- **How would your enemies describe you?** To your knowledge, you don't have any enemies. Mention someone in third grade who called you a brain.

- **You have one hour and access to all the printed matter in the world. What do you choose to read?** Theoretically, you have access to most of the printed matter in the world right now.

With that in mind, the best response is that you would pick up whatever you are currently reading.

• **What is the toughest question that you have been asked today? Why?** Mention a question that seemed bizarre at the time, something that you had never considered before, like "What flavor are you?" Chances are you'll have one of these questions in mind.

Partying Interviewers

Some interviewers, especially those called on infrequently, see the whole hiring process as a chance to party. The power trip, the fancy meals, and the cocktail receptions are all perceived as great fun, and the candidates (bright-eyed, bushy-tailed, and ready for anything) appear the perfect playmates. If one of these little devils happens to be the president of the corporation, it's fine to play along. But otherwise, these interviewers—who can lose a lot of respect around the office as a result of their antics—can bring you down with them.

At the end of the daylong callback sessions at my firm, we would have a reception for all of that day's candidates. At one such reception, one of the candidates was missing. Thinking he was lost, we commenced a manhunt that lasted about fifteen minutes. The exercise was halted abruptly when the candidate, wobbling and smelling of bourbon, stumbled into the reception room arm in arm with a young interviewer in a similar state.

The interviewer, who had taken a liking to the candidate, had decided that a few drinks at the bar downstairs would be a fine reward for a hard day of interviews. The interviewee, wanting to oblige, accepted the invitation and then found himself going drink-for-drink with his more-seasoned host. This didn't look good for either person, but it was, of course, the candidate who paid the price.

The moral of the story? Go out of your way to please each interviewer but not to the displeasure of the whole group. If a mischievous interviewer tries to corrupt you, it's probably not a trap; he just wants to have some fun. But unless that interviewer sits on the hiring committee, it's a dangerous gamble.

Meals

Most callback interviews involve a meal—usually either an interview lunch or a group dinner. The lunches are most frequently conducted two-on-one, and some attempt is made to discuss your interests and qualifications, short of bringing up your GPA and SAT scores. Few interviewers will bring your résumé to the table; be prepared to recall your history without it. Rarely will they, and never should you, use the lunch interview as an opportunity to raise any difficult points or unpleasant issues. Confrontation and food don't mix.

Group dinners, with their lighter atmosphere, are usually thought of as a chance to relax after a long, hard day. Every candidate who has a callback that same day will be present, along with most of the interviewers. Although you are not likely to be interviewed *per se*, don't think that you can let your guard down for a second. The head of recruiting will probably begin the dinner with a speech stating that "all the judging is over," but that simply will not be true. As a matter of habit, recruiters take candidates to dinner specifically in order to observe their social skills and group behavior. If there were nothing to be learned from the meal, the firm wouldn't pay for it.

With this in mind, certain obvious rules prevail. If you want to drink, don't drink a lot, and keep your wits about you. Don't try to be the life of the party, but don't sit quietly in the corner. Participate in conversations for most of the meal—not necessarily with an interviewer, but with *someone*. I wasn't impressed by people who bent my ear all evening, but a candidate had to make conversation to survive the dinner.

The candidates who fared worst during the dinners were the ones who, recognizing that they were being judged, tried too hard to impress. Unless you are usually a wallflower, a big-mouth, or a jerk, the best advice is to act natural and politely enjoy yourself.

There are, of course, other permutations of the candidate meal—group lunches, interview dinners, power breakfasts, etc. When you are uncertain of what you are getting yourself into, follow this rule: If you are the only candidate present, think of it as a relaxed interview and a chance to casually manifest your qualifications; if there are other candidates at the same table, think of it as an enjoyable meal where only your social skills are being tested.

Mealtime Etiquette

How you carry yourself at a meal is as important as what you say. Not only do you want to avoid disgusting the interviewer with unappetizing eating habits, but you also want to demonstrate that you can be trusted with a fork during a business meal. When you eat, don't think that your table manners aren't being observed quite closely.

We'll begin by assuming that you know how to eat a formal restaurant meal without making a fool of yourself. If you're not certain of the proper roles of the various forks and spoons, ask someone to teach you. Your bread dish will usually be on your left, your water and wine glasses on your right. If the napkins can't decide whom they belong to, wait and see what your neighbors do.

Don't worry about sticking out your pinkie when you drink tea, but sit up straight, put your napkin on your lap (folded in half with the crease toward you), keep your elbows off the table, and don't talk with your mouth full—easier said than done during an interview. I've found that taking small bites is the key to eating and carrying on a conversation simultaneously.

You should not begin eating until someone else does, even if everyone else's food is late. Don't pour your own wine unless you've served everyone else first. Men: If a woman joins the table, rise halfway out of your chair as she sits down. (Sexist? Perhaps, but ultimately appreciated.)

Avoid ordering the most expensive thing on the menu, but there is no need to order the cheapest dish unless it's something you really want. Don't spend a long time deciding, and once you've expressed a preference, don't change your mind. If your interviewer suggests something that you think you can stomach, try it.

Don't order spaghetti, onion soup *gratinée*, or any other intrinsically messy dish. I once ordered veal during an interview, which was fine, except it came on a bed of spaghetti. Rather than leaving a half-finished plate, I chose to eat the spaghetti, which wasn't easy. Spotting my difficulty, the interviewer (a rather youthful vice president) tried to get me to laugh, and succeeded. It was all in good fun, but the results were a bit messy and I didn't get the offer.

At lunch, beware of anything heavy or spicy that might make your afternoon interviews unpleasant. Also refrain from drinking alcohol at lunch, both for appearances' sake and to keep you on your toes. Iced tea and Perrier are much classier than cola or a root-beer float.

At dinner, alcohol can pose a difficult dilemma. A beer or glass of wine, if you want one, is rarely unacceptable, but don't be the only one drinking. And if you can feel the alcohol, it's time to stop.

A smart interviewer will ask you to order first, but if not, wait and see what the others choose to drink. If you have strong doubts, play it safe with mineral water. The only unforgivable move, aside from ordering a double scotch, is to ask for a beer, see that everyone else is staying dry, and then *change your order*. It's better to be a lush than a wimpy lush, and an unacknowledged mistake—if it's a mistake at all—is quickly forgotten.

The Committee Meeting

Most applicants have an over-romanticized idea of what goes on in the final recruiting committee meetings. While the mechanics vary from firm to firm, it is fair to say that these meetings are not all that exciting. Any drama that does arise comes from the fact that the committee members, often reduced to playing the role of a clerk, lustfully cherish any opportunity to influence the tide of the meeting.

The role of recruiting committee members has become increasingly clerical as the decision-making process has become more refined. Often using computers, companies succeed in quite literally turning candidates into numbers. Here's how the system worked at my firm:

Each applicant had been through more than a dozen interviews before the final decision was made. The interviewers ranged in rank from analyst (the position sought) to managing director. Each one had rated the candidates in a number of categories, such as those discussed in chapter 4, and had come up with an overall score. This score ran from 1 to 5, as follows:

1. unacceptable. Under no circumstances should this candidate be hired.
2. fair. I do not recommend hiring this candidate.
3. good. I would not object strongly to a hire.
4. hire. Possesses all of the necessary qualifications.
5. strong hire. One of the best candidates I have interviewed.

Some interviewers may have given the candidates pluses and minuses, but in any case each one's qualifications and performance were reduced to a single faceless digit. These digits were averaged to yield an overall score. We then put this information on a computerized spreadsheet that ranked the candidates from top to bottom.

In our selection meeting we looked at both overall ranking and range of scores. We automatically extended offers to the highest-ranked candidates, with the exception of those whose scores were not at all consistent. When we spotted a very low score on a highly ranked candidate, we pulled out the review sheets to find out why.

I remember one candidate who had received all 4s and 5s, except for a single 1. One of our interviewers, reading "Fluent in German" on the résumé, had asked him, in German, "Do you enjoy studying languages?", to which the candidate had responded, "What?" His single 1 didn't ruin his average, but it ruined his chances of getting hired.

The other instance in which we looked at the individual review sheets was when the candidate was sitting right on the margin of a hire. Those of us who had interviewed him would argue our cases, and the others would chime in with cocktail-party observations. This is when the job could get exciting; many of the things said could be grounds for libel suits if printed here, as I'm sure is the case with any recruiting committee. Our disputes, however, were usually resolved without coming to a vote, mostly due to the understood hierarchy of the people in the room.

The main philosophical question we faced was how low to stoop. Despite the apparent superiority of the candidates who had made it to the second round, we always seemed to have trouble meeting our quota. If we were looking to make twelve offers from a group of thirty candidates, we would invariably end up with only ten solid "hires." Unfortunately for the candidates, we would generally just lower our quota accordingly.

While we tried to maintain the semblance of a democratic process, we couldn't very comfortably hire a candidate who received a 2 from a managing director. At other firms, where there is no pretense of democracy, the final decisions are often made by the most senior interviewer, "counseled by" the other interviewers' scores. If you have a callback at a very small firm, or if the position in question is to be answering to only one person, you can expect a more one-sided decision-making process.

I have provided an overview of the decision-making process at my firm more to satisfy your curiosity than to provide you with the whole inside story—every company's process has its idiosyncrasies. If there is any universal rule to be learned here, it is that *all* of your interviews are important, but especially those with recruiting committee members and high-ranking professionals. Don't think that a twenty-two-year-old can't decide your fate, but don't take the real heavies lightly either.

The Expense Itemization

In order to reimburse you for the cost of your callback visit, most firms will request that you send them an itemization of your expenses. Although this itemization may not be received until after all decisions have been made, it allows you to display the sort of skills that will be expected of you on the job. Will it affect your chances? Probably not in a positive way: If they don't like you, it won't change their minds. But an extremely disorganized letter, or one with expenses of a questionable origin, can be enough to topple a decision that hangs in the balance.

Get receipts for everything you do and make sure they look official. Hotel rooms, transportation, and *reasonably priced* meals are all expected to be billed, but there is probably nothing else for which you should claim reimbursement. Resist the temptation to live it up on the company tab. Sixty-dollar dinners can be great, but they're not worth jeopardizing a thirty-thousand-dollar job.

The most businesslike method of submitting your expenses is to number your receipts, staple them all together (once), and clip them to a cover letter that includes a concise itemization. Unless you're told otherwise, address the letter to the recruiter who planned your trip. Stick to business, but include one sentence about enjoying your interviews. Don't be overly fastidious—you'll look like an anal-retentive time-waster—but take the opportunity to make it obvious that you're organized and responsible.

7

The Offer

Put It to Good Use

Once you have the offer, you might believe that there is no way you can mess up, but don't relax yet. There's plenty to be lost and plenty to be gained from this point onward. Aside from the main goal of making the right decision (which I'll discuss soon), you have to keep in mind how your actions and behavior can affect your life on the job. There's no doubt that you're firmly in the driver's seat by this point, but you've only just begun to make an impression on people who will be judging you all anew from day one on the job. Also, if you play your cards right, you can both begin to establish yourself in the firm "network," and squeeze a little something extra out of the company.

The Offer Itself

An offer can come from one day to six weeks after your callback interview. At my firm we prided ourselves on making offers the following day, but this was far from the norm of two weeks or so. Most companies will tell you during the callback what to expect, but don't be surprised if it takes longer. One thing is certain: If you don't have your offer within a month of the interview, you're probably on some sort of secret waiting list.

That's what happened to me at Merrill Lynch when I was a candidate. After three weeks of no news, I called them and got them to admit my status: If someone else turned them down, I'd get an offer. Of course, you can't expect all recruiters to be so honest.

Offers can come in the mail, but the better firms like to make them over the phone—both to show their enthusiasm and to gauge your response. You will typically be given details regarding salary, bonus potential, benefits, and starting date. Some callers may even ask for a decision on the phone, but if they do, it's probably a joke. No recruiter can expect you to act so quickly.

It's easy to get flustered by the thrill of an offer, so make sure you have all the facts straight before you hang up. The caller may be intentionally vague about certain details, and it's your responsibility to ask him to clear them up. While it's ridiculous to ask what annual bonus you'll receive, the mention of a bonus gives you the right to inquire about its possible range.

Continuing the Good Impression

How do you respond to the offer itself? There's nothing wrong with letting the recruiter know that you're happy about it, but direct that elation toward serious enthusiasm rather than wild celebration, at least on the phone. Aside from being turned down flat, nothing would disappoint my colleagues and me more than hearing the phone drop and the candidate run screaming to his roommates, "I got it! I got it!"

Don't confuse the "corporate bonding ritual" initiated here with the feelings of acceptance and warmth derived from a good fraternity or sorority rush. Despite your temporary good fortune, this remains the "dog-eat-dog" business world, and you shouldn't let your guard down at this point. As another example of how not to behave: It is in bad taste to ask the caller if any of your friends who interviewed with you also got an offer.

Do not expect the salary to be negotiable; it rarely is. Now and then a small firm might kick in a little extra to win a candidate, but this practice is unheard of when it comes to entry-level jobs at the large corporations. Don't ask about it unless you have strong suspicions, and prepare to be embarrassed when you do.

Never accept the offer right away, even if you're certain about it. *Within certain limits*, your future bosses are likely to most cherish the fish that was most difficult to land. As enthusiastic as you were about the firm during the interview, you are definitely entitled to let them know you have a *tough decision* on your hands. But a word of warning: It is a dangerous mistake to tell him that you have other offers that you don't, especially if you mention well-known firms, since most recruiters have friends working for the competition.

Before delaying for long, make sure that you fully understand the terms of your offer. Few firms are likely to say "Sign now or forget it," but many would like to be able to do so. What is more common, primarily at the post-MBA level, is the "evaporating offer," in which a substantial signing bonus diminishes week by week as you delay your decision. It is virtually impossible to get caught in one of these power plays without being warned first, however, so just be sure to keep your ears open.

Generally, the candidate is almost *expected* to politely ask by what date the firm wants a decision. If you do so and they respond with "Friday," it isn't poor manners to say something like, "I'm sorry, but would it be possible for me to have a bit more time? As enthusiastic as I am about the offer, this is a big decision for me, and I think that I shouldn't rush it." They'll understand, and they'll also be impressed by your maturity.

With the above in mind, however, don't hold out any longer than seems polite, unless you must. One month is typically enough time to make any decision. I held out for seven weeks before accepting my offer, and the only reason they didn't end up shooting me for it was that I had forewarned them. (I had other interviews scheduled for the following month.) If you have known commitments down the road that will delay your decision for more than a few weeks, give the firm a set date by which they can expect a definite response. Otherwise, you'll be a nuisance to each other: they for calling you continuously and you for wasting their time and effort.

There are other ways to be bothersome after you have an offer. Probably the worst of these is believing that a job offer entitles you to an endless chain of question-filled phone calls that prevent everyone in the office from working. Up to a point, such inquiry is expected, but more than a few candidates have crossed the line into the annoyance category, where all the hirer wants to do is renege on the offer. You'll be less likely to overdo it if you remember that the person you're annoying will be your superior when you eventually arrive at work.

That same advice will help you to avoid another common mistake: ego-trampling. As much as the person in charge of "selling" you wants to please you, generosity can quickly change to resentment if you make him feel at all like he has to beg. Because this is the one time during the process when he has to impress you more than you have to impress him, he is likely to feel a bit vulnerable. Never lord your offer over him; as sweet as he is to you, many a seller believes—some correctly—that you owe your good fortune to his kindness. Taking for granted someone who helped hire you is one sure way to get the cold shoulder.

To be safe, and sincere, you should give your interviewer the same respect after the interview as before. Too many candidates make the mistake of becoming too laid back after they've received the offer, treating the formality of the interview process as if it were some temporary charade. Don't—and it's been done—pop by the office, dressed in shorts, to say "Hi." If you visit, behave as if you're showing up for your first day of work.

Finally, when you make your decision, do it firmly and enthusiastically. No matter how much of a coin toss the choice ultimately was, let your employers know that you're with them 100 percent. It's fine to tell them that you had a tough decision to make, as long as you imply that you will never regret having made it. No one wants to work with someone who lets on that he would rather be somewhere else.

Getting Everything out of the Offer

Not only can you use your offer as a tool to establish yourself within the company, you must also use it to avoid getting cheated. Dealing with the second item first: All jobs are not created equal. Or, more specifically, all the different divisions or groups into which you may be placed are not equally advantageous places to work.

At my firm, we would hire through a single mechanism for an entire division, and then parcel out the new employees to a variety of quite distinct groups. An applicant hired through Corporate Finance could just as easily end up in International Finance, Short-Term Finance, Real Estate, or Mergers and Acquisitions. In my division, Public Finance, it was often a completely random choice whether a new hire went to work for the Health Care or the Housing Group. And it was of continuous amusement to me that so many recruits would allow themselves to be passively herded like sheep to one group or another, rarely attempting to have any influence on their own future.

It is easy to see why these people expressed no preferences—they didn't know the first thing about the different groups. Yet, had they made a greater effort, many would have discovered some things that would have interested them. For example, there were times when analysts in one group would be working twice as hard as in another. On the Corporate Finance side, analysts in Mergers and Acquisitions would often put in twenty-five more hours per week than their counterparts in Short-Term

Finance. This is the sort of thing that you might want to know.

So, without being a nuisance, find out as much as possible about your options before accepting the offer. If you decide that certain divisions appeal to you more than others, let it be known *before you sign.* When I accepted my investment banking job, I did it with the understanding that I was going to be placed in the Housing Group. Because I was polite about my preference, nobody was turned off, and my future bosses liked me all the more for choosing their division over the others.

Because so few people actually express preferences, there's almost always room to be placed where you want. Usually, a few careful hints such as, "I'd really love to work in the Housing Group," will earn you the guarantee you're looking for. Of course, if you find yourself having to insist, it's really quite acceptable to do so. Just ask straight out: "Do you think it would be possible for me to work in the Housing Group?" If you've got other offers, they'll take the hint.

As suggested, you can also use the offer to establish yourself as a *popular* employee long before you arrive on the job. Specifically, you can make friends by crediting certain people with your decision to work there.

The "selling" procedure varies from firm to firm, but there are almost always several individuals who stand to gain from your acceptance of the offer. At my company, certain professionals (myself included) were assigned the responsibility of "selling" three or four accepted candidates, and a tally was kept of our success. While no money changed hands, a mild competition resulted in which each candidate was worth a number of prestige points. At some firms, recruiters, like professional headhunters, actually receive a commission for each successful "sale."

Though this aspect of the process is beyond your control, that does not prevent you from using it to your advantage. Once you have a good idea of whom you hope to be working with, choose one of them to be your mentor. This person should probably be your future immediate superior or someone else whose favor you know you'll have to earn. Let him in on your decision-making process and make plain his positive influence on you. When you finally come to a decision, call this person and let him know first. Ultimately, your efforts will make your "mentor" look good, and you'll arrive at work with an appreciative friend.

Finally, an offer comes with certain wonderful perks, and you shouldn't allow your own sense of frugality, or humility, to prevent you from enjoying them to the fullest. Never *ask* to be flown anywhere, but if the firm offers you an all-expense-paid trip to The City, don't be shy about accepting their hospitality. Furthermore, understand that you're not the only one who enjoys fine French cuisine; accepting a lunch invitation will probably make your hosts happy as well. If you like being wined and dined and can maintain the proper balance of enthusiasm and decorum, then take whatever is offered.

Making the Right Decision

So many factors go into choosing among offers that there is no way I could address the topic completely here. Your concept of the ideal job should allow you to assemble a logical methodology for making an educated decision. Should you need help in putting together a decision-making model, you might consult any of the dozens of general career books available at most libraries.

The People Although these models can be useful—especially if you're not very good at thinking for yourself—most people end up making "gut decisions" based on which firm makes them feel the most comfortable, that is, where they like the people the best. This is as it should be—ultimately, it's the people who will determine whether you enjoy your job. However, most job-hunters err by judging the wrong people. A suave personnel worker or an enthusiastic "seller" has nothing to do with your day-to-day experience at the firm, and it's a mistake to let their charms influence your decision. Likewise, even with all the current talk about "collegial corporate culture," that concept may be foreign to the people who will be running your life.

Take the time to get to know your future superiors. Access the grapevine, discreetly, to find out what they're *really* like. It's worth the effort—one bad boss can ruin your whole experience.

The Long Term In all the excitement over starting salaries and fancy business cards, its easy to make another mistake: forgetting about the long term. While one job may initially seem more attractive than another, it may be quite inferior in terms of advancement opportunities. More importantly, a firm with great Christmas bonuses might have a lousy reputation that will permanently scar your résumé. And keep in mind that your résumé will continue to influence your fate, due to the ever increasing mobility of the job market. A tremendous amount of promoting occurs from one firm into another. Just as your summer employment was key in earning you this offer, so is this job most useful in earning your next.

The "Marine Attitude"   In choosing among offers, don't let your ambition make you masochistic. Though it is natural to want a challenging job, many candidates confuse slave labor with truly worthwhile activity. It is easy enough, amid all the talk of "excellence, dedication, and desire," to consider the most demanding job to be the best. Many people who make that error regret it later; the rest are workaholics.

Don't be carried away by that charismatic interviewer who promised to make a man (woman) out of you. You definitely had to play along during the interviews, but now is the time to step back and ask whether you have other interests besides work. "Being all that you can be" is indeed attractive, but trust me when I tell you that seventy-five-hour weeks and constant travel can get old pretty fast.

Perks   If being wined and dined is important to you, the interview process is likely to give a good indication, relatively speaking, of your life on the job. The company that gives you the best meals as a candidate will probably give you the most perks as an employee. But be aware that I'm speaking proportionately: In almost all cases, the luxuries you experience once you're hired will be much fewer than the interview process has led you to expect.

The best advice is to see through the perks to the job itself. You'll eventually find that job satisfaction comes from what you accomplish at the office rather than what you eat for lunch. All those frills can be a soothing compensation for an awful job, but they otherwise count for very little.

Security I decided to add these paragraphs when a number of my friends were fired from Wall Street after the latest "crash." You'd be surprised how many firms' hiring mechanisms keep cranking full speed ahead even while word circulates of imminent layoffs. The contraction of the securities industry was an unusual case: Most of those jobs were lost overnight. In your typical, less market-sensitive profession, cutbacks are much easier to anticipate. Yet poor management can result in your still getting a job offer from a firm that is actually one step away from bankruptcy.

Presumably, your preliminary research on future employers has alerted you to any existing warning signs, but you'd be smart to double-check. Don't confuse annual report rhetoric with articles in the *Wall Street Journal,* and don't assume that you're getting the straight scoop from the personnel office. Talk to someone at a competing firm, and use whatever business connections you've established to find out the "word on the street." While it is less work to assume that everything's intact, you don't want to have to start the whole job-hunting process over again.

Complainers Finally, if you've come across *anyone* during your interviews who was less than completely enthusiastic about the job or the company, get in touch with him. He may just enjoy complaining—or he may be the only honest person you've met. Take what he says with a grain of salt, but don't ignore it; you'll never get anywhere if you shy away from what you don't want to hear.

Decline Letters

I urge you not to skip this stage of the job-hunting process, largely because it's enjoyable. Also, it's a good way to set yourself up for the future—not the distant future, since these letters are rarely saved for very long, but the next year or so, or as long as you can make your favorable impression last.

It was surprising to discover, after observing the rigidity and apparent finality of the entire process, that there exists so much mobility from the final decision onward. Once you have worked your way into an industry, you are much more attractive to people within that industry. This means that switching jobs is much easier than finding the first one was. A fair number of my friends ended up changing firms rather quickly after being hired, some in as little as six months' time.

None of them planned to find their first jobs unsatisfactory, and neither will you, but it happens. What also may occur is that companies, finding themselves short-handed in the hiring off-season, will send out headhunters to raid other firms' new blood. Some, like mine, even conduct the campaign in-house— I was involved in a mid-year hiring push in which my division increased its analyst pool by 20 percent. In either case, it quickly becomes the question of *who knows whom* that determines whether your name comes up. If I had a friend at another firm who I knew was unhappy there, I threw his name into the hat. Likewise, any headhunter who called me about an opening, upon hearing my denial, would ask me if I knew of anyone else who might be interested. This is where maintaining connections at other firms comes in handy and why the decline letter is necessary.

You should address your decline letter to the person who was officially in charge of the recruiting process, both as a matter of proper procedure and because this is someone who is likely to be involved in any future employee-hunting. However, this should not stop you from reaffirming other contacts. In your letter, mention one or two people at the firm who were particularly helpful, especially the professional who was in charge of signing you. You may want to accompany the letters with a phone call or two as well.

The same principles apply in the decline letter as in the thank-you note. You may never speak to the recipients again, but you still want to establish a friendly rapport. If possible, credit your decision to some cause independent of your assessment of the company. Location is a good excuse, as is the existence of a special, unusual opportunity at your chosen firm. Mention your difficulty in making your decision, and generally say everything you can short of "check back with me in six months." An effective sample decline letter is shown opposite.

Hopefully you'll have no need to follow up on the decline letters you send, but good public relations is never a bad idea.

Sample Decline Letter

Dear Ms. Givings,

I would like to thank you again for the exciting offer to work at BigBank. It is certainly a thrill to have made it through your rigorous process. Unfortunately, I have made the difficult decision to accept an offer from the sales and trading division of BiggerBank. While many aspects of the position at your firm are perhaps preferable to the one I'm accepting, BiggerBank has offered me a spot on its Strictly Profit Desk, something that I find myself unable to turn down.

In some respects this decision goes against my "gut instincts," especially when I think about how at home I felt during my interviews at your firm. If the people who interviewed me are any indication, BigBank must be a very enjoyable place to work.

I'd also like to convey my appreciation to Mr. Dow and Mr. Jones for the wonderful lunch and for the helpful discussion. I can only hope that I too am able to eventually develop such a full understanding of the banking industry.

Thanks once more for all of your help, and I hope to see you again sometime soon.

Sincerely,

Ahab T. Job

Final Disclaimer

After you have read this book, a few general rules may stick out in your mind as the keys to a successful job search: Smile; be friendly; put yourself in the recruiter's shoes; and tell people what they want to hear. The final rule is an unfortunate one, and may cause you to think twice about the whole corporate recruiting scene. (Good.) However, if you are a less-than-perfect candidate, you need to appear perfect to get the job, and this may require some *creative presentation* of the facts.

Be careful, though: If you have to *lie* to get the job, then the job probably isn't for you.

Take some comfort in the fact that, with what you know now, the *right job for you* is well within reach.

Index